The Great I Am

Living The Abundant Life Through The New And Better Covenant

by: Dr. Lynn Hiles

Lynn Hiles Ministries P.O. Box 127 Great Cacapon, WV 25422

This book and all other books and materials by Dr. Lynn Hiles are available at www.lynnhiles.com or by phone at 304-579-5336.

For Worldwide Distribution Printed in the U.S.A.

ISBN 978-0-9839034-2-0

First Printing: 2020

DEDICATION

Sometimes the most important people on the planet are not the ones who stand in front of the crowds. Often, they are the ones who work tirelessly behind the scenes. They are the ones who never get recognition, credit or accolades from others. They are the support system and the nuts and bolts that keep the ministry going. They are just as vital to the body of Christ as any man or woman of God that stands in front of the crowd and receives recognition. Many times, the quiet wife who is not up front goes unnoticed, is pushed to the side or has unrealistic expectations put upon her by well-meaning people.

It is for this reason I want to dedicate this book to my wife, Joyce, for her undying support and incredible administrative gift. She manages my office and is gifted with organizational skills that I lack. She truly complements me. Without her there would be no Lynn Hiles Ministries. She is my closest, trusted confidant and my best friend. She is my biggest cheerleader and I love her dearly. I would not want to experience life without her. God surely hand picked her as a gift to me. We just celebrated our 44th wedding anniversary this year, 2020, on Valentine's Day.

When we began our journey together, we had no idea of the impact we would make on the world together. The greatest success is not always in who knows your name nor is it the books you have written or how many times you have been on television or the platforms from which you have preached. Our greatest achievement in life is raising a family that is passionately in love with Jesus and seeing his purpose fulfilled in the earth. I give most of the credit to my wife for what she poured into our two sons, Jeremy and Jason. Often, I was traveling, and she was at home raising the children alone.

Jeremy is the lead pastor of *Word That Frees* church in Winchester, Virginia, where our son Jason is worship leader. We have two wonderful daughters-in-law, Liza and Leslie. Jeremy's wife, Liza, is a medical doctor. Jason's wife, Leslie, is a chiropractor. We also have three wonderful granddaughters, Ellen Grace, Aspen Tabor, and Marina Lynn. They are the joy of our life. I dedicate this book to them and the generations to follow.

A special thanks to my son Jason who has helped take our ministry to another level with technology and his graphic design skills. For ten years now he has produced our national television program *Dr. Lynn Hiles - That You Might Have Life*. He has managed our website and our audio and video department that is reaching around the globe.

I also want to dedicate this book to our faithful partners who have empowered us to touch the world. Without you, none of this would be possible. We are deeply grateful.

ENDORSEMENTS

In the beginning of 2018 I had been invited to speak at a pastors conference. I watched an auditorium of worn out leaders weep tears of joy upon hearing the good news of God's unearned, undeserved grace. At the conclusion of my session I stepped off the platform to be met by someone asking if I might take a moment to meet a gentleman who had wanted to be introduced to me. As I looked over his shoulder, I saw Dr. Lynn Hiles. Instantly, I was overcome with humble tears, as this man's writings and television broadcast had profoundly shaped me as I embarked on my own grace journey. Little did this man know he had mentored me from afar and helped give me a language to the revelation of the New Covenant. Dr. Lynn Hiles has a unique ability to direct our attention and focus back to the one and only point: JESUS. His books are not littered with endless points to fill pages, but rather the One Point is woven throughout, constantly renewing our minds to our Source of joy, freedom and life. I know this newest book, THE GREAT I AM, will follow suit. So, pull down the safety bar, and throw your hands up as you take the ride of your life.

Pastor Ben Dailey

Calvary Church, Dallas, Texas

Author of: Limitless and Collide

Overseer of Gospel Circle of Churches and Ministries

The Seven I Am's written by Dr. Lynn Hiles expounds on the seven times in the gospel of John that Jesus says, "I Am".

Naturally we are presently dealing with the corona virus pandemic of 2020 which has affected the entire world and spiritually we are dealing with a darkness covering the minds of people all over the world.

This book will reveal to you who Christ is through the Seven I Am's

I am reminded of the scripture in Isaiah 25:7

Isaiah 25:7 And he will destroy in this mountain the face of the covering cast over all people, and the veil that is spread over all nations.

Isa 25:8 He will swallow up death in victory; and the Lord GOD will wipe away tears from off all faces; and the rebuke of his people shall he take away from off all the earth: for the LORD hath spoken it.

The question ask by Jesus to Peter;

Luke 9:18 Whom say the people that I am?

Luke 9:19 They answering said, John the Baptist; but some say, Elias; and others say, that one of the old prophets is risen again.

Luke 9:20 He said unto them, But whom say ye that I am? Peter answering said, The Christ of God

The writings of this book will encourage and bring you into the life of Christ and as with Paul, your spirit will yearn to know Him and the power of his resurrection. We need to know the only true God and Jesus Christ that we may have eternal life now.

Be ready for a transformation by the renewing of your mind. A change that takes place inside of your very being that brings forth a manifestation of his nature, from Adam to being in Christ. We become a doer of the word and not a hearer only. There is not a change only in our behavior but a change in our heart.

As you read the pages of this book you will experience abundant life through his name. You will realize he is much bigger than a ticket to heaven but the saving of our spirit, soul and body and the present reality of the Kingdom of God.

As John stated in chapter 6:63 It is the spirit that quickens; the flesh profits nothing: the words that I speak unto you, they are spirit, and they are life.

You are about to experience the empowering of the Holy Spirit and Heaven on Earth through the GREAT I AM

Pastor Galen Winebrenner
United Christian Temple
Uniontown, PA

CONTENTS

FOREWORD

I remember well the day my father backed the 'go cart' off the trailer and pushed it up into our yard. It was a gift! I had been the 'quasi leader' of a 'bicycle gang' of neighborhood boys that peddled and sweat our way through our daily lives. But now, I had been delivered from my bike and moved up into the world of 'go carts'! No peddling just push the gas and go.

A few days later I was quite a distance from my house when all of a sudden, my go cart sputtered and came to a standstill. Not knowing what I had been given, nor how it really worked, I got out and thought, "What a gift! This thing doesn't work"! So down the road I went, pushing my go-cart that wasn't 'going'.

After a few blocks I passed an older man that said to me, "I can give you some gas for that go-cart if you need it". Gas? No one had told me what 'sustained' my go-cart. He put the gas in the tank and we fired it up. Off I went, no longer having to 'push' what was meant to carry and sustain me.

When I first met Dr. Lynn Hiles, I was immediately aware of the gift that he was to the body of Christ. His incredible revelation and insight to living the abundant life through the finished work of Calvary and the new and better covenant we have in Christ, were revolutionary. I left his presence full of faith and freedom!

At the same time, I was aware of the agitation he could create in the hearts of people who are used to having to 'sweat and push their religious experiences' by human ingenuity and fleshly efforts! It can be quite confusing to have to 'work' for what was 'free'. Then to discover that religious systems have been the response of humanity to anything we don't understand about God. Inevitably we're going to abuse or be abused by anything we don't know the purpose or function of, including our relationship with God.

In the book you are holding The Great I Am, Lynn takes us on a journey of knowing Christ Jesus as more than just our Savior but also as the Source of our life the Zoe life … the abundant, overflowing life that is the essence of a relationship with the indwelling Christ.

One of the greatest tragedies in history is the devastation that comes from humanity listening to a 'lie' and believing that somehow we can obtain the limitless potential in our lives apart from His Life! He IS our Bread of Life, our Door, our Shepherd and so much more!

I encourage you to allow this book to become a light to your pathway, illuminating the revelation and possibilities of a "life hid in Christ". The light of Truth has always been present, even in the darkest days of history, but now, Dr. Hiles turns up the lumens allowing us to see the full revealing of the GREAT I AM!

Enjoy your journey … stop sweating and start living!

Bishop Tony Miller
Senior Pastor of The Gate Church, Oklahoma City, OK
Bishop of Destiny Fellowship of Churches

INTRODUCTION

Anyone who is a serious student of the Word will soon find that throughout the Scripture God speaks to us through types, shadows, and symbols. It is the language of the Spirit to communicate spiritual things to our natural minds. The Old Testament is Jesus concealed and the New Testament is Jesus revealed. In the volume of the book it is written about him. The pictures, types and shadows are the language that God uses to speak to us. For instance, we know that the Passover Lamb in the book of Exodus was a type and shadow of Christ, who is our Passover Lamb. Once you learn this language of the Spirit, it will become a key to open the Scriptures like never. They are powerful keys to understand and communicate God's purposes and his Kingdom.

The apostle John writes the purpose for his gospel in this verse:

But these are written, that ye might believe that Jesus is the Christ, the Son of God; and that believing ye might have life through his name. John 20:30-31 KJV

For far too many, the abundant life that was promised seems to be elusive, or it is postponed until you get to Heaven. However, Jesus himself declared, "I came that you might have life and have it more abundantly." Of course, that includes Heaven, but the Scripture also declares in the book of Deuteronomy, that God wants to give us as the days of Heaven on earth. This abundant life should be the light that attracts people to God.

In this book, we will explore the seven times in the gospel of John that Jesus says, "I Am." Every time He uses that phrase, it is always in contrast to something from the old covenant. For instance, they thought the bread that fell in the wilderness was the true bread, but Jesus says to them, "Your fathers ate manna in the wilderness and are dead, but I Am the true bread." They thought Moses and the law were the door into the sheepfold, but Jesus said to them, "I Am the door." They thought the corrupt shepherds of Israel were the true shepherds, but Jesus said, "I Am the Shepherd of the sheep." They thought that Israel was the true vine, but Jesus said to them, " I Am the vine, you are the branches." They thought their natural genealogy was the way to the father but Jesus said, "I Am the way, the truth, and the life."

According to the book of Corinthians, the old covenant was the administration of death written on stone tablets. That covenant did not produce life. It was a covenant of death. I believe what has robbed most Christians of enjoying the abundant life has been a performance-based Christianity based on the law of Moses trying to live out of the wrong covenant, or it is the mixture of law and grace. Paul calls the mixture of law and grace a perversion of the gospel. Jesus came to redeem us not just from sin but from the curse of the law. Religion is a thief that will rob you of life. Jesus did not come to offer us religion. He came to offer a relationship. A personal and intimate relationship with Him that will produce the abundant life. The gospel is not about a law you must keep. It's about receiving a life that will keep you. As you read the pages of this book, you will truly discover that faith replaces fear, and that through believing you will have life through His name. You will surely rediscover that Jesus removed the covenant of death and replaced it with the covenant of life. You will, without a doubt, rediscover that He is *"The Great I Am."*

CHAPTER 1
LIFE THROUGH HIS NAME

30 And many other signs truly did Jesus in the presence of his disciples, which are not written in this book: 31 But these are written, that ye might believe that Jesus is the Christ, the Son of God; and that believing ye might have life through his name. John 20:30-31 KJV

John the beloved has given to us one of the most incredible treaties of New Testament truth. He states his purpose for writing this book in the above scripture and that purpose is believing you might have life through his name. Life through his name can be a mystery or an enigma to many believers in this hour. What does it mean to have life through his name? In this book I plan to mine the hidden treasures and look at a few of the signs that Jesus gave his first century believers. What did he mean when he said abundant life? What does eternal life mean? To what do these signs point?

Signs along the highway usually post information as to what is ahead or what you should be aware of around the next curve. As I have studied this book, I realized that Jesus did nothing that was not significant. Everything he did pointed to an incredible revelation that he in fact was the promised Messiah and Israel's long-awaited King. Every miracle he did and every sign he demonstrated pointed toward the confirmation that he was in fact who the prophets foretold. Jesus came to fulfill the promises that God had made to Israel and to the world through the law and the prophets. Many of the scribes, Pharisees and religious rulers of his day did not grasp his message, nor did they recognize their King because he did not come in a fashion of which they were looking. They were waiting on the King to come with pomp and ceremony, only to find that their King came to them wrapped in swaddling clothes and laying in a manger. His beginnings were humble. He was not born in a palace. The people did not recognize the day of his visitation because he did not come in a way that fit their expectations. Is it possible today that many have missed the present reign of Jesus Christ because he does not fit our preconceived ideas of what his kingdom looks like? Is it possible that we are so enamored with a coming Jesus that we forgot about the one who lives and resides within us? Have we forgotten that he said I will never leave you or forsake you, even to the end of the world?

My primary focus in this book will be on the seven times that Jesus said, "I AM". Is it possible that Jesus was identifying himself in his union with God the Father whose voice thundered in the desert to Moses when he said, who must I say sent me to bring the children of Israel out of Egypt? The answer that boomed from the heavens said to tell them that "I am that I am" sent you. Seven times in the book of John Jesus says, "I am", establishing himself as the great I am and the leader of a new Exodus. In this book we will look at all seven times Jesus said, "I Am". Perhaps when I am finished it will create a faith in you that says, I believe. That faith will produce an incredible abundant life that is available to every true believer; the result being life through his name.

- Another Exodus -

Throughout the New Testament there is an Exodus theme. Did you ever wonder why baptism was such a big deal in the first century? Perhaps it was because when they came out of Egypt they were baptized in the sea. Then when they crossed over into the promise land, they crossed the Jordan River. In the mind of the first-century Jew standing there, they would have thought this is symbolizing another Exodus about to take place. As a matter of fact, one of the first things that happens in the book of Matthew is that John the Baptist identifies the true Lamb of God. As Jesus was walking down the bank of the Jordan River, John looked up and declared "behold the Lamb of God who takes away the sin of the world". It was the blood of the spotless Lamb applied to the doorpost of the Hebrew home that was the beginning of the first Exodus. John the Baptist identified the real Lamb and said to them, it is time for another Exodus, repent, for the kingdom of heaven is at hand. In other words, what you have been waiting for is now available to you if you can change the way you think. I wrote much about this in my book "From Law to Grace": A kingdom paradigm shift. I encourage you to read that book for an in-depth look at what took place in the Jordan. Another Exodus was at hand and now the last and final ultimate Lamb of God was on the scene. The question is, would they receive deliverance, or would they reject this incredible gift. Would they leave Egypt, or would they choose to remain in bondage because it was familiar to them? One greater than Moses had arrived. The leader of a brand-new Exodus, King Jesus, was about to bring them out of bondage that he might bring them into a different kind of promise land. I think the same question arises today in our hearts. Do we want deliverance from bondage? Can we lose our slave mentality and replace it with a sonship mentality? Under the old covenant you were slaves. In the new covenant we are sons.

I do not think it is an accident that in Luke, Moses and Elijah appeared to Jesus on the Mount of Transfiguration. It is on that mountain that the Scripture says,

30 And, behold, there talked with him two men, which were Moses and Elias: 31 Who appeared in glory, and spake of his decease which he should accomplish at Jerusalem. Luke 9:30-31 KJV

The Scripture says they talked to him concerning his decease. What is interesting to me is that the word decease in this text is the Greek word Exodus. In this verse the leader of the first Exodus is talking to the leader of the real Exodus concerning his impending death. Perhaps Moses and Elijah, which speak of the law and the prophets, realized that everything they had done by type and shadow was now being fully manifest in the spotless Lamb of Calvary, Jesus Christ. Perhaps they told him all the types and shadows of the old covenant sacrificial system were about to be fulfilled in his death, burial, and resurrection, and that he in fact was the leader of the new Exodus.

Much is written about this in my other books, so I will be brief in my summary here. I think it incredible that Moses only ever asked God for two things: let me see your glory and show me the promise land. Moses spent 40 years in Egyptian schools and would have been the heir apparent to the throne of Egypt, but he chose to suffer affliction with the people of God rather than enjoy the pleasures of sin for a season. The word sin in this text means to miss the mark. The mark he would have missed would have been his call to be a deliverer. One day he left the plushness of the palace and saw the condition of God's people in their bondage, and what he was born to do surfaced. He was born to be a deliver. My prayer is that this book helps many leaders find their destiny as they look on the condition of God's people, and true leaders realize that they too were born to be delivers. Moses spent the next 40 years in the backside of the desert learning to keep sheep. It was there that he had his first encounter with the great I AM. Then he went on a 40-year camping trip with people who did not want to go camping. They were not happy campers. In a moment of frustration, he failed to sanctify the Lord his God before the eyes of the people and smote the rock instead of speaking the word to the rock. God said to him, because you have failed to sanctify me in the eyes of the people you cannot go into the promise land. Perhaps the mistake of our generation is at the end of this wilderness journey. We are trying to smite the rock because we do not realize the rock has already been smitten, and that rock was Christ. We must declare that the rock Christ Jesus has already been smitten, and his smiting was my smiting. He was wounded for my transgressions. He was bruised for my iniquities. When we come to that understanding, water will gush out of that rock in a dry and thirsty land.

For many years it did not seem fair to me that after 120 years of service Moses would not be allowed to enter the promise land, especially since he only messed up one time. Behind my question was my own failures. If Moses did not make it, how could I ever measure up? Would I ever be allowed to enter the promise land? The Lord answered me and said, "I did that to show you that not even Moses, the mediator of that covenant, was going to make it in by the works of the law". It still had to be by the hearing of faith, so Moses died short of the promise land. The closest he came to it was that God hid him in the cleft of the rock. God said I am going to let all my goodness pass before you and you will see my glory, but you are only going to see my hinder parts. In the old covenant all you ever see is God's hinder parts. He seems to always be turning to walk away from you. But in the new covenant there is no variableness or turning of shadows. God will never turn his back on you. He will never leave you nor forsake you. God also allowed Moses to see the promise land from a distance. Scripture says that God buried him in a place where nobody knows to this day. It also says that the devil fought with Michael for the body of Moses. I asked the Lord why did the devil want the body of Moses? His answer to me was that the body of Moses spoke of more than just his physical body, but the entire body of the law. If he could have had the body of Moses, he could have used it as a weapon of condemnation against you for ever. Remember, Satan is the accuser of the brethren and what he uses to accuse you is an antiquated law. But in the new covenant no weapon formed against you can prosper. Any tongue that rises against you in judgment or condemnation, you will utterly condemn because your righteousness is of me saith the Lord. Then the Lord said to me, "I'm going to tell you where Moses is buried. He is in the tomb of Joseph of Arimathea, the same place I buried you". If you cannot find Moses, then you cannot find your old man either. You were crucified with Christ and your baptism signifies that you are on your way in this new Exodus to this new covenant promise land.

For almost 1500 years the prayer request of Moses was ringing throughout the corridors of glory. It was haunting God. His prayer request was legitimate. *Let me see your glory. Show me the promise land.* It was on the Mount of Transfiguration that Moses and Elijah appeared to Jesus. Perhaps they came down Jacob's ladder and when they saw Jesus, they realized that glory is not smoke in a corner. Glory is found in the face of Jesus Christ. He was the image of the invisible God. He was the great I AM. It was in that same moment that Moses and Elijah realized that the promise land is not a place, it is a person. Hebrews 4 declares to us that the promise land is rest in the finished work of Jesus Christ. For in Christ all of God's promises are yes and amen. Christ is the glory of God and he is our promise land. It is in him, that we live and move and have our being. It is through faith in his name that we have this incredible abundant life.

They spoke to him concerning his decease. Remember the word decease means Exodus. Do you see it? The leader of the first Exodus was talking to the leader of the real Exodus. Now the promise land was standing in front of them in the person of Jesus Christ. The time was at hand. God wanted to bring them out of Egypt and into a promise land of rest in his finished work.

- A Different Kind of Egypt -

Perhaps the bondage that God wanted to bring them out of this time was a spiritual bondage. Please note this Scripture:

8 And their dead bodies shall lie in the street of the great city, which spiritually is called Sodom and Egypt, where also our Lord was crucified. Rev. 11:8 KJV

I believe a careful study of this whole chapter will lead you to believe that the two witnesses in this chapter are a type of Moses and Elijah. They represent the law and the prophets, making their testimony against the great city. I have studied this text for years and it never dawned on me, because I read so quickly over the verse, that it states our Lord was crucified in the city which is spiritually called Sodom and Egypt. First, our Lord was not crucified in Sodom or Egypt. He was crucified in Jerusalem, the centerpiece of Judaism and the old covenant law. It was then that I began to realize that the Holy Spirit was taking his finger and pointing to the place where our Lord was crucified, calling it Egypt. Most of my life I was raised to believe that Egypt was whatever we decided was worldly for sin. I am not saying that cannot be a bondage as well. What I am saying is that the Holy Spirit is being specific to point out that the centerpiece of Judaism and the old covenant is what he called Egypt. In this new Exodus what God wanted to do was bring a nation of Israel out of the bondage of an old covenant system that had made slaves out of them. Remember, under the old covenant you were servants and slaves. In the new covenant you are sons, and since you are a son you are an heir of God and

18

joint heirs with Christ Jesus. It is only when we can truly identify what Egypt really is, that we participate in this new Exodus and truly find life through his name. Jesus, the true Lamb of God, the night before his decease gathered the 12 disciples in an upper room and said to them, with great desire have I kept this Passover with you. When he took the bread and broke it and said, this is my body which is broken for you and this cup is my blood of the new covenant, what he was saying to the 12 disciples is, you will never have to kill another Lamb again. This Passover is the final Passover and the real Exodus out of Egypt and its religious bondage has begun!

Please do not be like the Israelites who were so used to slavery that they did not know what to do with freedom. They continued to have a desire to go back to the diet in Egypt. I find in this hour. Many do not want to be set free from the bondage of religion. They like the fact that they have taskmasters that tell them how much to give, how much to go to church, how to behave, how many bricks to make and what the rules are, etc. For that kind of life, you do not need to develop a relationship with God, because you have rules. The basic mindset of most American Christians is simply, give me the basic rules for what it takes to go to heaven, and I am happy with that. But in this new Exodus, he will take us by the hand and teach what it means to walk in the Spirit. We will once again know the reality of what it means to walk with God in the cool of the day in Eden's misty garden. I have written much about the garden in my other books, so I will be brief here.

The Scripture says in Genesis, the heavens and the earth were "finished". Right in the middle of a finished work, God places a man in a garden and says, all you must do is guard and keep this garden. Guard and keep the finished work. Your only job is to throw your feet out of bed in the morning and say, just another day in Paradise, and get up and walk with God in the cool of the day. Live out of the divine supply of that relationship. That my friend is the life that Jesus came to restore back to us. The Scripture says they that are led by the spirit are the sons of God. The contrast is with what used to lead you as rules on rocks or, if you will, the law of Moses. Now you are being governed by the Holy Spirit living inside of you, as Jesus himself has now become the keeper of the garden. He is guarding and keeping his finished work. We as co-heirs with him must guard it as well. For we are God's garden. We are God's husbandry. Song of Solomon declares we are a garden enclosed; a spring shut up in a fountain sealed. For me, there is nothing to go back to. I refuse to go back to the whips and chains of an Egyptian slave system. It was for freedom that Christ set us free. We are no longer to be entangled in the yoke of slavery.

I am not suggesting that we trade the bondage of religion for the bondage or slavery of sin, or of substance abuse or some other thing that controls our life. I am talking about a freedom in Christ that will give you back your life; a life lived out of a promise land of rest in the finished work of Jesus Christ. The outflow of that life is that we become a land flowing with milk and honey. A lot of deeply profound things could be said about milk and honey. But if I said to you, I am going to give you a land that flows with milk and honey, that simply means I am going to give you the best life on the planet.

*18 Here it is in a nutshell: Just as one person did it wrong and got us in all this trouble with sin and death, another person did it right and got us out of it. **But more than just getting us out of trouble, he got us into life!** 19 One man said no to God and put many people in the wrong; one man said yes to God and put many in the right. 20 All that passing laws against sin did was produce more lawbreakers. But sin didn't, and doesn't, have a chance in competition with the aggressive forgiveness we call grace. When it's sin versus grace, grace wins hands down. 21 All sin can do is threaten us with death, and that's the end of it. Grace, because God is putting everything together again through the Messiah, invites us into life — a life that goes on and on and on, world without end.*

*1 So what do we do? Keep on sinning so God can keep on forgiving? 2 I should hope not! If we've left the country where sin is sovereign, how can we still live in our old house there? 3 Or didn't you realize we packed up and left there for good? That is what happened in baptism. **When we went*** *under the water, we left the old country of sin behind; when we came up out of the water, we entered into the new country of grace — a new life in a new land!* That's what baptism into the life of Jesus means. *4 When we are lowered into the water, it is like the burial of Jesus; when we are raised up out of the water, it is like the resurrection of Jesus. 5 Each of us is raised into a light-filled world by our Father so that we can see where we're going in our new grace-sovereign country. 6-7 Could it be any clearer?* Our old way of life was nailed to the Cross with Christ, a decisive end to that sin-miserable life — no longer at sin's every beck and call! *What we believe is this: 8 If we get included in Christ's sin-conquering death, we also get included in his life-saving resurrection.* Rom. 5:18 - 6:1-8 MSG

Do you see it? He did not just get us out of trouble, he got us into a life; an abundant life, not a bondage to religion, nor a bondage to sin. We have received free life, a new life in a new land. We now live in Graceland and Adam has left the building. Our old man was crucified with Christ. We are also raised in the power of his life-saving resurrection.

Where You Are Headed
- Does Not Look Like Where You Came From -

*9 and that you may prolong your days in the land which the Lord swore to give your fathers, to them and their descendants, 'a land flowing with milk and honey.' 10 **For the land which you go to possess is not like the land of Egypt from which you have come, where you sowed your seed and watered it by foot, as a vegetable garden**; 11 but the land which you cross over to possess is a land of hills and valleys, which drinks water from the rain of heaven, 12 a land for which the Lord your God cares; the eyes of the Lord your God are always on it, from the beginning of the year to the very end of the year.* Deut. 11:9-12 NKJV

What an amazing promise. Could it be any better than a land that flows with milk and honey? He will prolong your days in the land that you go into possess. It sounds to me like the good life on every level. This was the intention and heart of God for his people. Notice what he says in the

21

above verse about the land that you are going in to possess. "It is not like the land of Egypt", because when you lived in Egypt you had to sow your own seed and water it yourself. You had to work the garden. You had to sweat, labor, and serve the Egyptians. It was a land full of works and no rest, slavery and not sonship. You had to work your garden and carry the water from the Nile River. But where you were headed does not look like where you came from! Sometimes I think people have gotten so used to bondage that they do not know how to act in freedom. They love the familiarity of how it used to be in the good old days. Change is a difficult thing, especially for those who have been steeped in religious bondage their whole lives. Freedom to them sounds very scary. It sounds like it is too good to be true. They think that those of us who are teaching freedom are preaching heresy. But my friend, it is time for an Exodus. It is time to leave the bondage in the flesh pots of Egypt. It is time to walk away from all the legalism that has robbed you of life. It is time to spoil the Egyptians and begin your journey toward the promise land where you will live in houses you did not build and eat from vineyards you did not plant. You will enter into his finished work, trusting God to send the rain of heaven and to keep his promise. Being in Christ means we are the land for which the Lord God cares. We are in the land that the rain of heaven falls upon; a land for which the Lord our God cares. We are in Christ and in Christ all of God's promises are yes and amen. Christ and his finished work are our promise land in the new covenant.

21 That your days may be multiplied, and the days of your children, in the land which the Lord sware unto your fathers to give them, as the days of heaven upon the earth. Deut. 11:21 KJV

Could it be any clearer? God's intention and desire is to give us as the days of heaven on earth! I do not know about you, but that sounds like an exceeding great and precious promise to me. Could it be possible that we could walk in the days of heaven on earth? I believe that is what John the Baptist was declaring in Matthew chapter three when he said, repent, the kingdom of heaven is at hand. To many believers, when you talk about the kingdom of heaven, they think you are talking about where we are going when we die. However, a careful reading of all the Gospels will become clear that the preaching of the gospel of the kingdom of heaven was not about otherworld stuff. It is about *this* world stuff. It is about living in righteousness, peace, and joy in the Holy Spirit right now and right here. It is about living under a new form of government called the Holy Spirit. It is parables about stewardship. It is about faithfulness. It is about being faithful over little so that you can have authority over cities, etc. It is about God sending his Messiah to rescue and save his creation. It is about being co-laborers with God in his ongoing rescue mission, bringing about new creation. It is about God answering the prayer of Jesus when he said, your kingdom come, your will be done in earth as it is in heaven.

Make no mistake about it. I am not saying that there is not a heaven when you die. I am simply saying you do not have to wait until you die to receive the days of heaven on earth. You simply must believe. In believing you will have life through his name. It is sad to me that most of what is preached over American pulpits is teaching people to prepare for what happens after they die instead of training them how to reign in life right now. We should be teaching how to be the salt and light that we are called to be. The life that it produces will be the light that attracts men to the kingdom.

I was raised on a lot of teaching about the kingdom. However, most of what was taught back then was that you access the kingdom through old covenant righteousness. Since it was accessed through old covenant righteousness, the kingdom was always somewhere out in our distant future. It was like a carrot being dangled in front of a rabbit. We were always on the brink, always looking for a breakthrough. However, I realized that new covenant righteousness is not based on my performance but based on a gift. See Romans 5:17. It put the kingdom well within my reach. Everyone is in a different spot in their journey, so I am not being critical of where people are currently. I am just saying many of my kingdom friends have no understanding of grace with the new covenant. On the other hand, many of my grace new covenant friends have no understanding of the kingdom. I do not think it has to be either/or. I think both held in a careful balance will produce the manifestation for which we are looking.

I was reminded of this verse:

20 And when he was demanded of the Pharisees, when the kingdom of God should come, he answered them and said, The kingdom of God cometh not with observation: Luke 17:20 KJV

The kingdom does not come through your careful observances. It reminds me of the apostle Paul in this verse:

*9 But now, after that ye have known God, or rather are known of God, how turn ye again to the weak and beggarly elements, whereunto ye desire again to be in bondage?10 **Ye observe days**, and months, and times, and years. 11 I am afraid of you, lest I have bestowed upon you labour in vain.* Gal. 4:9-11 KJV

This was Paul's stern rebuke to the church in Galatia for going back under the law and returning to Old Testament observances. These Scriptures are telling you that the kingdom of God is not accessed through old covenant observances. Remember from above, the land where you are going in to possess, does not look like Egypt from whence you came. It is not about your works and labor. It is about what he has accomplished through his finished work to give us access to the days of heaven on earth.

If you have read the whole chapter of Deuteronomy 11, it says that the days of heaven on earth are predicated upon whether you keep all the commandments. The answer to that question is probably a resounding no. As a matter of fact, Romans chapter 3 tells us there is none righteous, no not even one. Not even Moses the mediator of that old covenant made it in by the works of the law. With that being said, it almost seems as if the days of heaven on earth are not within your reach. But we must remember that Christ is the end of the law for righteousness to everyone who believes. It is based on faith and faith alone that we now have access to this grace. It is through believing that we have life through his name. Let us compare these Scriptures in Deuteronomy with the Scriptures in Romans chapter 10 where the apostle Paul changes some of the wording.

24

*10 If thou shalt hearken unto the voice of the Lord thy God, to keep his commandments and his statutes which are written in this book of the law, and if thou turn unto the Lord thy God with all thine heart, and with all thy soul. 11 **For this commandment** which I command thee this day, it is not hidden from thee, neither is it far off. 12 It is not in heaven, that thou shouldest say, Who shall go up for us to heaven, and bring it unto us, that we may hear it, and do it? 13 **Neither is it beyond the sea,** that thou shouldest say, Who shall go over the sea for us, and bring it unto us, that we may hear it, and do it? 14 **But the word is very nigh unto thee, in thy mouth, and in thy heart, that thou mayest do it.** Deut. 30:10-14 KJV*

*10 Brethren, my heart's desire and prayer to God for Israel is, that they might be saved. 2 For I bear them record that they have a zeal of God, but not according to knowledge. 3 **For they being ignorant of God's righteousness, and going about to establish their own righteousness, have not submitted themselves unto the righteousness of God.** 4 **For Christ is the end of the law for righteousness to every one that believeth.** 5 For Moses describeth the righteousness which is of the law, That the man which doeth those things shall live by them. 6 But the righteousness which is of faith speaketh on this wise, Say not in thine heart, **Who shall ascend into heaven? (that is, to bring Christ down from above:)** 7 **Or, Who shall descend into the deep? (that is, to bring up Christ again from the dead. 8 But what saith it? The word is nigh thee, even in thy mouth, and in thy heart: that is, the word of faith, which we preach;** 9 That if thou shalt confess with thy mouth the Lord Jesus, and shalt believe in thine heart that God hath raised him from the dead, thou shalt be saved. 10 For with the heart man believeth unto righteousness; and with the mouth confession is made unto salvation. 11 For the scripture saith, Whosoever believeth on him shall not be ashamed. 12 For there is no difference between the Jew and the Greek: for the same Lord over all is rich unto all that call upon him. 13 For whosoever shall call upon the name of the Lord shall be saved. Rom. 10:1-13 KJV*

Do you see it? In Deuteronomy he says, "this commandment" is not far from you. It is not in heaven that you would say, who will go up for us to heaven and bring it to us, that we may hear it and do it? Notice the difference in Romans chapter 10 where Paul changes the wording. He replaces the words of this law by saying, who will go up to heaven for us, that is to bring down Christ from above. Do you see it? He replaces the doing of the law with the work of Christ. Notice in Romans chapter 10, for Christ is the end of the law for righteousness to everyone who believes. It is through faith in his name that we have access to this life. Remember, that is the purpose of the book of John. He said these things are written that you might believe that Jesus is the Christ, and that believing you would have life through his name.

Compare the next verse of Deuteronomy chapter 30, neither is it beyond the sea that you would say who will go over the sea for us and bring it unto us that we may hear it and do it. In the Deuteronomy passage it is about your performance. It is about *you* being able to do it. But in the Romans passage it is about the fact that Christ *already* did it on your behalf. In Romans chapter 10 it says, who will descend into the deep. The word deep in this text could be translated sea. It is a direct quote of Deuteronomy chapter 30. In the Romans passage he did not descend into the deep to bring to you the words of this law. He descended into the deep to bring up Christ again from the dead. You see he was delivered for your offenses but was raised for your justification. His death, burial and resurrection are what gives you access to the days of heaven on earth. It is through faith in his name that we enjoy this incredible abundant life.

In the Deuteronomy passage above he tells them that the word of the law is nigh them, even in their mouth. But in the Romans passage, it is the word of faith that is in our mouth and not the words of the law. The word of faith that we preach is not about how to get a bigger house or money or whoever dies with the most stuff wins. Let me also say that I am not opposed to the blessing of God, nor am I against prosperity. However, that is not the goal of this Scripture. If we seek first the kingdom of God and his righteousness, then all these things are added to us. They are the fringe benefits of believing in his finished work. The basis upon which we receive this according to Romans chapter 10 is that if we confess with our mouth the Lord Jesus and believe in our heart that God has raised him from the dead, we will be saved. Whoever believes in him will not be ashamed. He then goes on to tell them that this is not exclusive to the Jews. That is, to whosoever will call upon the name of the Lord, they will be saved. How exciting. How wonderful. What was once out of our reach is now within the grasp of anyone who will dare believe. Receiving this abundant life is no longer based on your performance. It is based on the person and work of Jesus Christ. Do not be like Israel in the first century. Do not go about to establish your own righteousness on basis of your works. That only leads to frustration and disappointment. It is hope deferred that makes the heart sick. It is the lie that tells you that you can only have this abundant life when you get to heaven. Believe it is available to you right now.

CHAPTER 2
THE LIFE OF THE COMING AGE

16 For God so loved the world, that he gave his only begotten Son, that whosoever believeth in him should not perish, but have everlasting life. 17 For God sent not his Son into the world to condemn the world; but that the world through him might be saved. John 3:16-17 KJV

This Scripture is probably one of the most quoted in the Bible. Pretty much everyone knows it by heart. Sometimes I think we are so familiar with it that we may be missing something right in front of our eyes. Let me preface what I am about to say by telling you that I do believe that eternal life includes going to heaven when you die. I also believe it is much more than that. I think that it may have carried a much broader implication to the first-century audience to which it was first spoken. This word everlasting comes from a Greek word *aionios*. It is from the Greek root word *aion*.

NT:165

<START GREEK>ai)w/n

<END GREEK> aion (ahee-ohn'); from the same as NT:104; properly, an age; by extension, perpetuity (also past); by implication, the world; specially (Jewish) a Messianic period (present or future):

KJV - age, course, eternal, (for) ever (-more), [n-] ever, (beginning of the while the) world (began, without end). Compare NT:5550.

NT:166

<START GREEK>ai)w/nios

<END GREEK> aionios (ahee-o'-nee-os); from NT:165; perpetual (also used of past time, or past and future as well):

KJV - eternal, for ever, everlasting, world (began).

(Biblesoft's New Exhaustive Strong's Numbers and Concordance with Expanded Greek-Hebrew Dictionary. Copyright © 1994, 2003, 2006 Biblesoft, Inc. and International Bible Translators, Inc.)

Once again, let me say that I believe that eternal life includes going to heaven when you die. However, I also believe that everlasting life was activated in you the moment you believed. You received the life that is afforded to you by believing in his name. Note in the above definition that the word aion is the Greek word for *age*. It especially speaks of a Jewish messianic period. (present or future). It began in the first century and continues to increase throughout all generations. Of the increase of his government and peace there will be no end. It also carries with it the idea of being perpetual, hence the idea that it lasts beyond your physical life. Thus, in the mind of the first-century Jew who would have been expecting a messianic age or period, he may have been thinking that this Scripture is much more than a ticket to heaven. It is the promise of the life of the coming age. Let us look at a few Scriptures where this Greek word for *age* is translated. We will see that this word very clearly has to do with an age. Our King James Bible did us a great disservice because it translated the word age several different ways. One of them is the word *world*.

*4 Who gave himself for our sins, that he might deliver us from this present evil **world**, according to the will of God and our Father*: Gal. 1:4 KJV

In this verse the word *world* is the exact same Greek word that is translated in John 3:16 as everlasting. Except here you can clearly see that he was talking about the present evil age that was fading from the scene, namely, the old covenant age. Let us look at the same verse in another translation.

*3 Grace to you and peace from God the Father and our Lord Jesus Christ, 4 who gave Himself for our sins, that He might deliver us from this present evil **age**, according to the will of our God and Father*. Gal. 1:3-4 NKJV

Do you see it? He came to deliver us, not from the world as being the globe, but from a present evil age.

This is my favorite end of the world Scripture.

*26 For then must he often have suffered since the foundation of the world: but now once in the **end of the world hath** he appeared to put away sin by the sacrifice of himself.* Heb. 9:26 KJV

Compare this verse with a more correct translation.

*6 He then would have had to suffer often since the foundation of the world; but now, **once at the end of the ages, He has appeared to put away sin by the sacrifice of Himself**.* Heb. 9:26-27 NKJV

Do you see it? These words when translated properly will shift the way we think. For the world that was passing from the scene was not a cosmic collapse of the globe. It was the end of an age, namely, the old covenant age. Let us look at another one.

*24 And Jesus went out, and departed from the temple: and his disciples came to him for to shew him the buildings of the temple. 2 And Jesus said unto them, See ye not all these things? verily I say unto you, There shall not be left here one stone upon another, that shall not be thrown down. 3 And as he sat upon the mount of Olives, the disciples came unto him privately, saying, Tell us, when shall these things be? and what shall be the sign of thy coming, **and of the end of the world**?* Matt. 24:1-3 KJV

3 Now as He sat on the Mount of Olives, the disciples came to Him privately, saying,"Tell us, when will these things be? And what will be the sign of Your coming, and of the end of the age?" Matt. 24:3 NKJV

Context and proper hermeneutics are everything. A text out of context is just a con. I am afraid we have been conned often. I am not saying we did it on purpose. Well-meaning preachers and people have made the mistake due to incorrect translations. We can have the best intentions and still be wrong.

In the above verses the context is that Jesus is speaking to a first-century audience as he was standing in front of beautiful temple buildings. He was prophesying the destruction of the temple and the end of the Jewish age. He prophesied the end of the old covenant age and the birth of the messianic period or age. He was not prophesying a cosmic collapse or the end of the world as a global destruction. He was declaring the collapse of the old covenant sacrificial system with the centerpiece of Judaism being their temple and their city. Remember, in Chapter I Egypt was identified by the Holy Spirit as the city which is spiritually called Sodom and Egypt. This was also where our Lord was crucified. Our Lord was not crucified in Egypt. He was crucified in Jerusalem. It was the very centerpiece of animal sacrifice and old covenant rituals. It was the end of their world. It is not the end of ours.

Jesus answered the question as to when this would take place in Matthew 24:34-35 when he said, "Assuredly, I say to you, this generation will by no means pass away till all these things take place. Heaven and earth will pass away, but my words will by no means pass away."

Jesus was setting a time text. He was declaring to them that all the prophecy he gave up to this point would certainly occur within that generation. I have heard some prophecy teachers tell us that Jesus did not mean the generation that was alive and well when he gave the prophecy. They teach that it is the generation that is alive and well that sees all these signs. Let us look at the context of the usage of the same word *generation*. It is used in Matthew 23 when Jesus says to the scribes and Pharisees:

*32 Fill up, then, the measure of your fathers' guilt. 33 Serpents, brood of vipers! How can you escape the condemnation of hell? 34 Therefore, indeed, I send you prophets, wise men, and scribes: some of them you will kill and crucify, and some of them you will scourge in your synagogues and persecute from city to city, 35 that on you may come all the righteous blood shed on the earth, from the blood of righteous Abel to the blood of Zechariah, son of Berechiah, whom you murdered between the temple and the altar. 36 Assuredly, **I say to you, all these things will come upon this generation**. Matt. 23:32-36 NKJV*

He was talking to a generation alive and well on planet earth when he gave that prophecy. Within 40 years of this prophecy all of it came to pass when the Romans destroyed the temple and the city. It occurred within that generation. It did in fact happen within that first generation. All these signs were fulfilled including tribulation, martyrdom, wars and rumors of wars, earthquakes, etc.

Often people ask me if this text could have a double fulfillment. I do not think so. Mainly because Matt. 24: 21 says, for then there will be great tribulation such as has not been since the beginning of the world until this time, **nor ever shall be**. The fact that he said to them, let him that is in Judea flee into the mountains, ought to be a huge clue to us that he was not talking about catastrophes on a global level. We do not live in Judea. It was specific to that region. He was talking about something that would occur in their world while they were still alive.

Why would a prophecy be given to those standing there that had no relevance to them? Remember, audience relevance is everything. To all the first-century Jews, and especially believers, they knew this would occur in their lifetime. Jesus told them, when you see Jerusalem compassed with armies you will know that it is near at the door. This was one of the major signs of his coming in judgment. When the Romans surrounded the city, they backed off for a short season and every believer that heard the prophecy of Jesus left the city of Jerusalem and fled to a place called Pella. Not one believer died in the siege of Jerusalem. They knew this prophecy was relevant to them. That should be incredibly good news to anyone with an open heart. What if you do not have hell on earth in your future? What if all of this is not in your future, but your past?

As a matter of fact, he tells them that famines, wars, earthquakes, and all the various upheavals prophesied was only the beginning of sorrows. Several other translations say *birth pains* instead of sorrows. It was the end of an old covenant age, but the birth pains of a new day were upon them. Only those who endured until the end would be saved. The end of what, you might ask. It was the end of the age of the law. Mankind was not just saved so they can go to heaven, but to endure to the end so that the salvation that was ready to be revealed in the last time would be given to them. They would be saved from the curse of the law. Jesus was made a curse for us.

They were not only saved *from* something they were also saved *for* something. That *something* being participators in the ongoing spread of the kingdom of God with its offer of abundant life. They were also saved from the destruction of the Romans. Salvation is a vast subject and cannot be confined to simply mean I have got my ticket to heaven. Once again, I do believe salvation includes heaven as final destination, but it is much bigger than that. It is deliverance for spirit, soul, and body.

- Birth Pains -

In Romans eight Apostle Paul talks about the suffering of his present time, not being worthy to be compared with the glory that shall be revealed in us. He goes on to declare that the whole creation was groaning and travailing. Birth pains were upon the entire creation because the coming age would be a life lived in the context of sonship. Jesus defined life eternal in John 17:3 like this; and this is life eternal, that they might know the only true God and Jesus Christ whom thou hast sent. The life of the coming age was a life lived in relationship with God as Abba, living out a father-son relationship instead of a servant mentality. Romans eight has so many times been preached out of context to try to justify our own individual suffering. However, Paul was not talking about suffering sickness or the various things we would call suffering. That is not to minimize any suffering that people are experiencing. But that is not what this text is talking about. He was talking about the fact that he hazarded his life every day for the sake of the gospel. He was in prison. He was snake bit. He was beaten. As a matter of fact, the text where he said I die daily was not talking about dying to his old nature. He was talking about the fact that he faced physical death every day of his life by the persecution of both Jewish leaders and Roman rulers. He was under the threat of constant imprisonment and death in the arenas. He was declaring that his suffering was not worth being compared with the glory that was about to be revealed. The whole creation would be brought into a glorious liberty of the sons of God. There are only a few things I think worth suffering and dying for and one of them is freedom. In this context we see Apostle Paul saying the suffering that we are going through in order to preach this gospel of freedom and liberty will not only set us free from the bondage of corruption, but set the entire creation free into the glorious liberty. What glorious liberty? It is the glorious liberty of living life free from the law and in the context of sonship. It is living life by the indwelling Holy Spirit working in us and through us. That was the birth pains upon the first-century church hearing these words. Today, even in the most legalistic church in the world, we are much freer than they were in the first century under the law. It was a bondage. It was a system of slavery. But it was for freedom that Christ set us free, no longer to be enslaved with the yoke of slavery.

27 Jesus resumed talking to the people, but now tenderly. "The Father has given me all these things to do and say. **this a unique Father-Son operation, coming out of Father and Son intimacies and knowledge. No one knows the Son the way the Father does, nor the Father the way the Son does. But I'm not keeping it to myself; I'm ready to go over it line by line with anyone willing to listen.** *28 "Are you tired? Worn out? Burned out on religion?* **Come to me. Get away with me and you'll recover your life**. *I'll show you how to take a real rest. 29 Walk with me and work with me — watch how I do it. Learn the unforced rhythms of grace. I won't lay anything heavy or ill-fitting on you. 30 Keep company with me and you'll learn to live freely and lightly."* Matt. 11:27-30 MSG

Do you see it? You will recover your life! The real gospel will give you back your life. Religion will rob you of life. That is what Jesus declared in this Scripture. He was not talking to drug dealers and prostitutes on the street. He was talking to people who had been involved in this religious system their whole lives. He was talking to people who had been under the yoke of slavery in bondage to the old covenant system. He is inviting them to be yoked together with him to learn the unforced rhythm of grace. He was inviting them into a unique father-son relationship. He was inviting them into the life of the coming age.

*12 So don't you see that we don't owe this old **do-it-yourself life one red cent**. 13 There's nothing in it for us, nothing at all. **The best thing to do is give it a decent burial and get on with your new life.** 14 God's Spirit beckons. There are things to do and places to go! 15 This resurrection life you received from God **is not a timid, grave-tending life. It's adventurously expectant, greeting God with a childlike "What's next, Papa?"** 16 God's Spirit touches our spirits and confirms who we really are. We know who he is, and we know who we are: Father and children.* Rom. 8:12-16 MSG

How powerful! This life that he offers us is not a grave-tending life. It is an exciting life of adventure and expectancy. That should make you shout, "what's next, Papa"?

- Adam or Christ -

Many years ago, the spirit of the Lord said to me, you must decide to whom you are going to preach. Either you are going to preach to Adam and the old man, or you are going to preach to the new man. If you are preaching to the old man Adam, you are going to have to preach behavior modification with all its sin management programs from the old covenant. The old covenant was given to modify the behavior of the old creation. It was a message of conformity. The new covenant was given to the new man to mature and develop him in his new identity as a son or daughter of God. The new covenant is about transformation. The apostle Paul said in Romans 12 be not *conformed* to this world but be ye *transformed* by the renewing of your mind. If you are under the old covenant you are being *conformed*. If you are in the new covenant you are being *transformed*. If you are being conformed, you are trying to change by superimposing a set of rules that are external. You are trying to change from the outside in. If you are being transformed, there is a metamorphosis that is taking place inside of you as you are being changed from the inside out. This change is not from heartache to heartache or from misery to misery, but from glory to glory even as by the spirit of the Lord. Remember in the verse above it says, we know who he is, and we know who we are: father and children.

The renewing of your mind does not mean you learn to memorize Scripture. It means that you must constantly renew your mind with your new identity. Renew your new life in a new land where God himself has taken up his abode within you. Make no mistake about it, those of us who teach grace desire to see change in the life of the believer. However, how that occurs is what is in question. Are you being *conformed* or are you being *transformed*.? Are you an old creation or a new creation? Are you in Adam or are you in Christ? The powerful truth is that Jesus did not come just to die *for* you. He came to die *as* you. He came to give you death to who you were in the old creation. Not only did he come to give you death to your old nature, but moreover to give you a resurrected life. He brought a new life in a new land. That is what happened in water baptism. You were buried with him in baptism and when you came up out of the water, it was an Exodus out of the old covenant, out of the old man, and out of the old age. You became dead to the law by the body of Christ. Therefore, you should be married to another, even to him who is raised from the dead, that you should bring forth fruit unto God. See Romans 7:4. We were born of the spirit and the water. It was identification with his death, burial, and resurrection. It was our Exodus out of Egypt and out of the old creation.

- Upon Whom the Ends of the Ages Had Come -

*10 Moreover, brethren, I do not want you to be unaware that all our fathers were under the cloud, all passed through the sea, 2 **all were baptized into Moses in the cloud and in the sea**, 3 all ate the same spiritual food, 4 and all drank the same spiritual drink. For they drank of that spiritual Rock that followed them, and that Rock was Christ. 5 But with most of them God was not well pleased, for their bodies were scattered in the wilderness. 6 Now these things became our examples, to the intent that we should not lust after evil things as they also lusted. 7 And do not become idolaters as were some of them. As it is written, "The people sat down to eat and drink, and rose up to play." 8 Nor let us*

36

commit sexual immorality, as some of them did, and in one day twenty-three thousand fell; 9 nor let us tempt Christ, as some of them also tempted, and were destroyed by serpents; 10 nor complain, as some of them also complained, and were destroyed by the destroyer. 11 Now all these things happened to them as examples, and they were written for our admonition, **upon whom the ends of the ages have come**. 1 Cor. 10:1-11 NKJV

In the above Scripture, the apostle Paul was reminding the first-century church at Corinth that everything that happened to the children of Israel under Moses was an example to them of the real Exodus to whom Jesus was now leader. In the old covenant they were baptized into Moses in the cloud and in the sea. In the new covenant we are baptized into Jesus Christ, the mediator of a better covenant. We are baptized in water as an identification with his death. We are baptized in the cloud on the day of Pentecost.

Everything that happened to them by type and shadow under Moses was now being played out in the new covenant. The old covenant was Jesus *concealed*. The new covenant is Jesus *revealed*. The old covenant was the *shadow*. The new covenant is the *substance*. The old covenant was *literal*. The new covenant is *spiritual*. Under Moses they saw a physical lamb taken out from the sheep and the goats and the blood put on the doorpost of their homes. In the new covenant John the Baptist points at Jesus and says, right there is the real Lamb of God. They *were* delivered by the blood in Egypt. We *are* delivered by the blood of Jesus in the new covenant from a different kind of Egypt. In Exodus they were baptized into Moses in the sea. In the new covenant we are baptized into Christ in water baptism. In the old covenant, exactly 50 days after they left Egypt, they came to the foot of Mount Sinai where God gave them the law. Now fast forward to the new covenant in Acts two, exactly 50 days after Jesus the real Lamb of God is crucified. They were in an upper room and were baptized in the cloud. In Acts two it says, when the day of Pentecost was fully come. The word Pentecost means 50, because Pentecost was exactly 50 days after Passover. This time God did not give them the law. He gave them the Holy Ghost. The Holy Ghost is to the new covenant what the law was to the old covenant. The reason preachers will not preach this is because they do not really believe the Holy Ghost can do what he said he could do. I am convinced that the old covenant is full of demands and the new covenant is full of supply. Under the old covenant it was rules on rocks with all kinds of demands. In the new covenant he gives us the supply of the indwelling Holy Ghost who writes his law on our hearts. Under Moses he gave them manna to eat. In the new covenant Jesus said, I am the true bread that came down from heaven. Under Moses they lifted up the serpent in the wilderness. In the new covenant Jesus declares, even as Moses lifted up the serpent in the wilderness so must the son of man be lifted up and I if I be lifted up from the earth will draw all men unto myself. Do you see it? The old covenant was the shadow or the type. In the new covenant Jesus is the fulfillment of what these types and shadows were about. We will now explore in depth this transition from natural to spiritual. Jesus himself uses these pictures on the road to Emmaus when he walked with them after his resurrection.

*27 **And beginning at Moses and all the prophets, he expounded unto them in all the scriptures the things concerning himself.** Luke 24:27 KJV*

The conversation may have gone like this: *Jesus may have said to them; Do you remember the Lamb that was taken out from the sheep and the goats? That was a picture of me. Do you remember the rock that was smitten? That rock was me. Do you remember the bread that fell from heaven? That bread was a picture of me?* We will explore a lot of this in depth as we look at the seven times that Jesus says, "I Am" in the gospel of John. Every time he says that, it is always in the contrast to something they were focusing on in the old covenant. For instance, Jesus would say your fathers did eat manna in the wilderness and they are dead, but "I Am" the true bread that came from heaven. In other words, you ate the natural bread, but that is not the true bread. I am the true bread. One was natural, the other was spiritual.

- A Different Kind of Temple -

Let me give you another example. In the first part of the gospel of John Jesus enters the temple and casts out all those who bought and sold doves, etc. He then tells them, destroy this temple and in three days I will raise it back again. Their carnal minds went out of the safety zone. They went on to tell him how many years it took them to build that physical temple. However, Jesus was not talking about the physical temple. He was talking about the temple of his own body. As a matter of fact, what he said there was one of the things that got him crucified. However, Jesus was talking about spiritual things and they were talking about a physical temple. In other words, Jesus was saying to them, you think this is the temple. This is not the temple. I am the real temple of God. I am the Bethel, the place where the Angels of God ascend and descend. I am the real house of God. I am the new temple. That is why the first temple had to be removed. God was moving out of the building and into a man. God finally found the man he was looking for in Isaiah 66.

*66 Thus saith the Lord, The heaven is my throne, and the earth is my footstool: **where is the house that ye build unto me? and where is the place of my rest**? 2 For all those things hath mine hand made, and those things have been, saith the Lord: **but to this man will I look**, even to him that is poor and of a contrite spirit, and trembleth at my word. Isa. 66:1-2 KJV*

God was finally realizing his dream when he said let them build a house so that I can dwell among them. It was through this new temple that God could finally dwell among us and in us because we are the body of Christ. We also are lively stones that are fitly framed together to build a habitation for God through the spirit. Apostle Paul said it like this, what, do you not know your body is the temple of the Holy Ghost. John the revelator set it like this...

I heard a voice thunder from the Throne: "Look! Look! God has moved into the neighborhood, making his home with men and women! They're his people, he's their God. Rev. 21:3-4 MSG

39

Oh, yes, God has moved into the neighborhood and property values just went up. When God moves into the neighborhood, he starts a major renovation program to make all things new. As a matter of fact, that is his mission. It is to make all things new and to bring about new creation. For that to happen an old creation must be removed. An old heaven and an old earth must pass away, and a new heaven and a new earth must replace it.

Ask a first-century Israelite what this verse means, and he would tell you it means the removal of their temple. For their temple was the place where heaven and earth met together. It was where God and man came together. It was the centerpiece of their old covenant. It was where animal sacrifice was made. Jesus was about to replace that system. Jesus would be the ultimate sacrifice and he would be the new temple. He would be God's Bethel, the place where Angels of God ascended and descend. He would be the location where heaven and earth would meet because he was human and divine. He was very God and very man. He was the interface that connected heaven and earth.

He was prophesying the removal of this natural temple when he said, not one stone will be left upon another. An old heaven, an old earth and an old covenant were about to pass from the scene, and a new heaven and a new earth were about to come on the scene. A brand-new temple, a brand-new bride and a new heaven and a new earth were coming. An old Jerusalem, the city spiritually called Sodom and Egypt, was about to be trampled underfoot by the Romans. A new Jerusalem was coming on the scene: the bride, the lamb's wife.

35 Heaven and earth shall pass away, but my words shall not pass away. Matt. 24:35 KJV

If heaven and earth have not passed away, then we are still under the law according to this verse.

18 For verily I say unto you, Till heaven and earth pass, one jot or one tittle shall in no wise pass from the law, till all be fulfilled. Matt. 5:18 KJV

A first-century Israelite would not have thought of a cosmic collapse of the planet, nor the destruction of heaven. After all, what could be wrong with heaven? He would have thought of the destruction of the temple and the removal of the old covenant. Their temple was like a microcosm of the universe. When John the revelator said there was no more sea, he was not talking about the ocean drying. He was talking about the removal of the brazen laver, or as Solomon called it, the brazen sea. The following is an excerpt from the writings of Josephus, the first-century historian.

The Temple was the gate of Heaven The following is an excerpt from the Works of Josephus. One of the most recognized historians.

\BOOK FIVE - From the Coming of Titus to Besiege Jerusalem, to the Great Extremity to which the Jews were reduced\Chapter 5 - A Description Of The Temple\§24 [5.24]\ - BOOK FIVE - From the Coming of Titus to Besiege Jerusalem, to the Great Extremity to which the Jews were reduced\Chapter 5 - A Description Of The Temple\§25 [5.25]

4. As to the holy house itself, which was placed in the midst [of the inmost court], that most sacred part of the temple, it was ascended to by twelve steps; and in front its height and its breadth were equal, and each a hundred cubits, though it was behind forty cubits narrower; for on its front it had what may be styled shoulders on each side, that passed twenty cubits further. Its first gate was seventy cubits high, and twenty-five cubits broad; **but this gate had no doors; for it represented the universal visibility of heaven, and that it cannot be excluded from any place. Its front was covered with gold all over, and through** it the first part of the house, that was more inward, did all of it appear; which, as it was very large, so did all the parts about the more inward gate appear to shine to those that saw them; but then, as the entire house was divided into two parts within, it was only the first part of it that was open to our view. Its height extended all along to ninety cubits in height, and its length was fifty cubits, and its breadth twenty. But that gate which was at this end of the first part of the house was, as we have already observed, all over covered with gold, as was its whole wall about it; it had also golden vines above it, from which clusters of grapes hung as tall as a man's

height. But then this house, as it was divided into two parts, the inner part was lower than the appearance of the outer, and had golden doors of fifty-five cubits altitude, and sixteen in breadth; but before these doors there was a veil of equal largeness with the doors. It was a Babylonian curtain, embroidered with blue, and fine linen, and scarlet, and purple, and of a contexture that was wonderful. Nor was this mixture of colors without **its mystical interpretation, but was a kind of image of the universe; for by the scarlet there seemed to be enigmatically signified fire, by the fine flax the earth, by the blue the air, and by the purple the sea; two of them having their colors the foundation of this resemblance; but the fine flax and the purple have their own origin for that foundation, the earth producing the one, and the sea the other. This curtain had also embroidered upon it all that was mystical in the heavens, excepting that of the [twelve] signs, representing living creatures.**

5. When any persons entered into the temple, its floor received them. This part of the temple therefore was in height sixty cubits, and its length the same; whereas its breadth was but twenty cubits: but still that sixty cubits in length was divided again, and the first part of it was cut off at forty cubits, and had in it three things that were very wonderful and famous among all mankind, the candlestick, the table [of shew-bread], and the altar of incense. **Now the seven lamps signified the seven planets; for so many there were springing out of the candlestick. Now the twelve loaves that were upon the table signified the circle of the zodiac and the year;** but the altar of incense, by its thirteen kinds of sweet-smelling spices with which the sea replenished it, signified that God is the possessor of all things that are both in the uninhabitable and habitable parts of the earth, a quote from The Works Of Josephus[1] complete and unabridged.

1. The Works of Josephus, Complete and Unabridged, new updated edition, copyright 1987 by Hendrickson Publishers, Incorporated.

Heaven and earth were about to pass away. An old temple was about to be replaced with the living Temple. The old covenant was about to be replaced with the new covenant. Old Jerusalem was about to be replaced with new Jerusalem. An old creation was about to collapse as God was giving birth to a brand-new creation. Yes, the first-century church at Corinth was the generation upon whom the ends of the ages had come. Note, it was the ends of the ages, plural. It was the back end of the old covenant age and the front end of the new covenant age. See the picture below where these two ages overlap there was a 40-year transition period. Jesus gave the great prophecy in Matthew 24 somewhere around 30 A.D. and the temple was destroyed in 70 A.D. It was a 40-year transition period just like the children of Israel spent 40 years in the wilderness. Many of the first-century Jews did not leave this spiritual Egypt. They did not apply the blood of the Lamb to their houses. Jesus had fulfilled every requirement of the law when he cried out from the cross, "It is finished." But for the next 40 years the writer of the book of Hebrews says the law was fading away. It would find its end in the destruction of the temple. For the next 40 years everything that happened under the old covenant by type and shadow would find its fulfillment in Christ. He was the true Lamb. He was the bread that came down from heaven. He was the fulfillment of the serpent on the pole. Jesus himself said, even as Moses lifted the serpent in the wilderness, so must the son of man be lifted. If I be lifted up from the earth, I will draw all men unto me. He spoke this concerning what death he would die.

Yes, the life of the coming age was upon them; a life lived in the context of the new covenant. The entire book of Hebrews was written to Hebrews some 30 years into the new covenant. The writer continues to affirm the concepts that are laid out in this chapter. The book of Hebrews is a treaty about what is better about the new covenant than the old covenant. It has better blood. It has a better priesthood. It has a better faith. It has a better temple. It has a better sacrifice. It has a better city, etc. The book itself starts out by saying, God, who at sundry times and in times past spoke to us by the prophets, hath in these last days spoken to us by his Son. The last days he was referring to was not the last days of this age. It was the last days of the old covenant age. The life of the coming age was now available to anyone who would enter in.

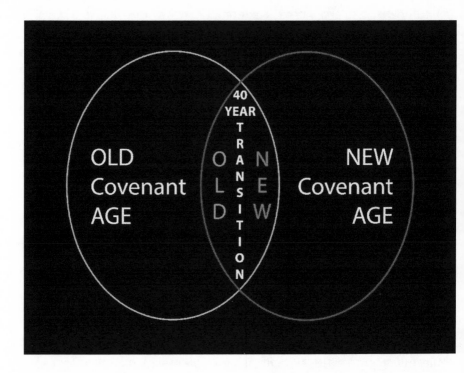

I do not want to spend much time on the subject of eschatology, or the study of end time events at this point because that is not the subject of this book. My objective in this chapter is to get you to focus on spiritual things; to have a paradigm shift from a natural carnal viewpoint to see things the way Jesus was teaching them in their spiritual fulfillment. I pray that the eyes of your understanding will be enlightened as we look at the seven times that Jesus says, "I AM" in the gospel of John.

CHAPTER 3
I AM THE LIGHT OF THE WORLD

*1 In the beginning was the Word, and the Word was with God, and the Word was God. 2 The same was in the beginning with God. 3 All things were made by him; and without him was not any thing made that was made. 4 **In him was life; and the life was the light of men.** 5 And the light shineth in darkness; and the darkness comprehended it not.* John 1:1-5 KJV

The gospel of John does not begin like the other Gospels. It does not begin with the genealogy of Jesus. It begins with a striking comparison with the creation story in the book of Genesis. I believe the reason for this is the story of Jesus is the offer of life not just to the nation of Israel. It was for all of creation. It was God revealing his intention to include both Jews and Gentiles in the new creation. The life of the coming age was being offered to both Jew and Gentile. This was the fulfillment of the prophecy of Isaiah 9:1-2.

*12 Now when Jesus had heard that John was cast into prison, he departed into Galilee; 13 And leaving Nazareth, he came and dwelt in Capernaum, which is upon the sea coast, in the borders of Zabulon and Nephthalim: 14 **That it might be fulfilled which was spoken by Esaias the prophet**, saying, 15 The land of Zabulon, and the land of Nephthalim, by the way of the sea, beyond Jordan, **Galilee of the Gentiles**; 16 The people which sat in darkness **saw great light**; and to them which sat in the region and shadow of death light is sprung up. 17 From that time Jesus began to preach, and to say, **Repent: for the kingdom of heaven is at hand.** Matt. 4:12-17 KJV*

Note he did not say the kingdom is way off in the distant future. He said it is at hand. It is within your reach. He was talking to a first-century audience. Remember, in the first chapter I wrote a bit about the kingdom of God, not being about otherworld stuff. It was about this world stuff. It was a new life in a new land with a new form of government called the kingdom of God. Let us compare the Scripture in John one with the

Scripture in Genesis one.

1 In the beginning God created the Heaven and the earth. 2 And the earth was without form, and void; and darkness was upon the face of the deep. And the Spirit of God moved upon the face of the waters. 3 And God said, Let there be light: and there was light. 4 And God saw the light, that it was good: and God divided the light from the darkness. Gen. 1:1-4 KJV

In Genesis one the earth was without form and void and darkness was upon the face of the great deep. Chaos was the order of the day. But right amid chaos and darkness, the spirit of God moved upon the face of the waters. Chaos is the end of what is not working any longer. It can also be the beginning of something brand-new. Probably many of us came to God amid darkness and chaos in our lives. It was at that point God began to move and the spirit of God hovered like a chicken sitting on an egg to give birth to a new creation. Much like he did in the book of Genesis in his first creation, it was amid this darkness that God said, "let there be light". When the light came it divided the light from the darkness and order began to develop.

John chapter one connects us to the Genesis motif by saying, in the beginning was the word and the word was with God and the word was God. The same was in the beginning with God. "Let there be light" took on new meaning, because light was now the life of Jesus that would be the light to all men. Much like the Genesis motif, John writes his gospel amid chaos. Something was not working any longer, namely the old covenant. God was about to change the order by bringing light into the world through the life of Jesus Christ. The chaos of an old covenant was about to be replaced with the order of the new covenant, and the kingdom of God was about to be established through the Holy Spirit. God's spirit was once again hovering over the darkness, but this time he was about to give birth to new creation. When you follow the story of Genesis you can almost see the steps of recovery. God simply declares light and when he does it divides the light from the darkness. Jesus was about to draw a line in the sand in his earthly ministry because he was going to expose the darkness of the passing evil age. Much of the darkness was religious darkness. He

46

was dividing the light from the darkness. He would do that through the manifestation of his life.

*12 For we wrestle not against flesh and blood, but against principalities, against powers, against the rulers of the darkness of this world, **against spiritual wickedness in high places**.* Eph. 6:12 KJV

In Genesis, the spirit of God moved upon the FACE of the water. It was as if God leaned over the balcony of glory and the reflection of his face was seen in the waters. In the gospel of John his image was seen in the FACE of Jesus Christ. He was the image of the unseen God. As you follow the story in Genesis, once the light begins to come, God begins to divide the waters and then the dry land appears. Then the earth begins to bring forth grass, fruit trees and all kinds of life. There is a progression to the creation until ultimately, he is finished; there is a man in his image with dominion.

- The Man in the Mirror -

I am reminded of a passage in James one, where he talked about a man who was a hearer of the word and not a doer. He was like a man who beheld his natural face in a glass and straightway he forgot what manner of man he was. That man became a hearer of the word and not a doer. In that passage the word for natural face is the Greek word *Genesis*. In other words, a man who is a hearer of the word and not a doer is like a man who beheld his Genesis face, that is the face of his new creation. Then forgets who he is in the new creation. When we go our own way and forget that the man in the mirror is the new man, we become hearers of the word and not doers. If we look into the perfect law of liberty, not the law of Moses, and continue there, we will become a doer of the word and not a hearer only.

In the movie The Lion King the young lion who was born to reign had become the victim of identity theft. He forgot he was the son of the King. He forgot he was born to reign. As a result, he lived in the wilderness with warthogs and meerkats singing Hakuna Matata. He believed the lie that his father had left him. One day a prophet found that young lion and said

47

to him, your father never left you. Many in this hour believe Father God has forsaken us, but he will never leave you or forsake you. He lives in you. He lives in me. That prophet took the lion to the water. I like to think of that water as the water of the word. When he looked into the water, he thought he saw his own reflection. He said to the prophet, "that's my reflection". But the prophet said, look deeper my son...look within. Your father never left you. He lives inside of you. When he looked back at the water, he realized the face of his father was reflected in the water. In Genesis one the spirit of God moved on the face of the water. God simply put his reflection in the water so that we can discover who we are in him. We were born to be his image bearer. When the young lion was reminded of his identity, a roar emerged from his lips that sounded like the roar of a mighty lion. It was at that moment that he realized he was born to reign. He said to his associates, we are headed back to pride rock to take our rightful place and begin to reign again. What was once a waste howling wilderness will become a garden of God.

The old covenant is a government of condemnation. The new covenant is a government affirmation. The old covenant tells you what is wrong with you. The new covenant tells you what is right. The old covenant tells you who you are in Adam. The new covenant tells you who you are in Christ. The old covenant steals your identity. The new covenant gives you back your true identity. I am afraid that most of God's children have been victims of identity theft. As a result of old covenant preaching a veil is placed over your face so you cannot see the end of what is abolished. But the new covenant removes the veil so that you can look in the mirror and see God face to face. It is in beholding his face that we are changed from glory to glory even as by the spirit of the Lord. Jesus is the image of the invisible God and now we can behold him face to face and be changed.

9 If the Government of Condemnation was impressive, how about this Government of Affirmation? 10 Bright as that old government was, it would look downright dull alongside this new one. 11 If that makeshift arrangement impressed us, how much more this brightly shining government installed for eternity? 12 With that kind of hope to excite us,

48

*nothing holds us back. 13 Unlike Moses, we have nothing to hide. Everything is out in the open with us. He wore a veil so the children of Israel wouldn't notice that the glory was fading away — 14 and they didn't notice. They didn't notice it then and they don't notice it now, don't notice that there's nothing left behind that veil. 15 Even today when the proclamations of that old, bankrupt government are read out, they can't see through it. **Only Christ can get rid of the veil** so they can see for themselves that there's nothing there. 16 Whenever, though, they turn to face God as Moses did, God removes the veil and **there they are — face to face**! 17 They suddenly recognize that God is a living, personal presence, not a piece of chiseled stone. And when God is personally present, a living Spirit, that old, constricting legislation is recognized as obsolete. We're free of it! 18 All of us! Nothing between us and God, our faces shining with the brightness of his face. And so we are transfigured much like the Messiah, our lives gradually becoming brighter and more beautiful as God enters our lives and we become like him. 2 Cor. 3:9-18 MSG*

In him was life and the life was the light of men. That light was about to shine in darkness much as he did in Genesis. The spirit of God was moving on the face of the water and the new creation was being formed. The process had begun. The earth was about to bring forth after its kind, just like it did in Genesis. The final thing in the progression of his creation ended with a man in his image, with dominion. The chaos was about to give way to order. The word was made flesh and dwelt among us (and we beheld his glory, the glory as of the only begotten of the Father, full of grace and truth.) He was full of grace and truth, not law and judgment. John 1:17 says, for the law was given by Moses, but grace and truth came by Jesus Christ. Do you see the contrast? He was saying to them, you thought Moses was the light, but he is not the light. I am the light of the world. The light was shining in the darkness, but the darkness comprehended it not. He came to his own and his own received him not. But to as many as received him, to them gave he power to become the sons of God. The life of the coming age was a life lived in the context of sonship. It is a life lived out of a father-son relationship. That relationship was now available to both Jew and Gentile and to whoever would call on the name of the Lord. Let us look at the context of the first time Jesus said, "I Am".

- The Woman Caught in Adultery -

*1. Jesus went unto the mount of Olives. 2 And early in the morning he came again into the temple, and all the people came unto him; and he sat down, and taught them. 3 And the scribes and Pharisees brought unto him a woman taken in adultery; and when they had set her in the midst, 4 They say unto him, Master, this woman was taken in adultery, in the very act. 5 Now Moses in the law commanded us, that such should be stoned: but what sayest thou? 6 This they said, tempting him, that they might have to accuse him. But Jesus stooped down, and with his finger wrote on the ground, as though he heard them not. 7 So when they continued asking him, he lifted up himself, and said unto them, He that is without sin among you, let him first cast a stone at her. 8 And again he stooped down, and wrote on the ground. 9 And they which heard it, being convicted by their own conscience, went out one by one, beginning at the eldest, even unto the last: and Jesus was left alone, and the woman standing in the midst. 10 When Jesus had lifted up himself, and saw none but the woman, he said unto her, Woman, where are those thine accusers? hath no man condemned thee? 11 She said, No man, Lord. And Jesus said unto her, Neither do I condemn thee: go, and sin no more. 12 Then spake Jesus again unto them, saying, **I am the light of the world:** he that followeth me shall not walk in darkness, but shall have the light of life.* John 8:1-12 KJV

The first time Jesus says, "I Am" it is right after he utters these words, "neither do I condemn thee: go, and sin no more".

In the above verses Moses gave the law, but grace and truth came by Jesus Christ. In this text the scribes and Pharisees brought to Jesus a woman caught in adultery. They said to him, Moses in the law commanded us that such should be stoned: but what sayest thou? They were operating in the chaos and darkness of an old covenant system without any grace or truth. Mercy was not on their minds. It is amazing to me that this woman was supposedly caught in the very act of adultery. My

50

question is where was the man with whom she was committing adultery? He was probably standing there with a rock in his hand. It is also amazing to me that they all knew her address. See, the problem with old covenant is it can point out your problem, but it has no supply of grace to empower you to live above your weakness. Note also in this Scripture the scribes and Pharisees are not interested in helping this woman. They are interested in accusing Jesus because he is exposing the utter futility of a works-based system that has no power to change the heart. The law can change your behavior, but only grace can change the heart.

- He Stooped Down -

The first thing Jesus did in response to their accusations was to stoop down. I see some powerful imagery here. His response to her failure was to stoop down. He lowered himself and took on the human condition. He became what I am so I could become what he is. The son of God became the Son of Man so that the sons of men could become the sons of God. Look at this incredible verse:

3 God went for the jugular when he sent his own Son. He didn't deal with the problem as something remote and unimportant. In his Son, Jesus, **he personally took on the human condition,** *entered the disordered mess of struggling humanity in order to set it right once and for all. The law code, weakened as it always was by fractured human nature, could never have done that. The law always ended up being used as a Band-Aid on sin instead of a deep healing of it. 4 And now what the law code asked for but we couldn't deliver is accomplished as we,* **instead of redoubling our own efforts, simply embrace what the Spirit is doing in us.** Rom. 8:3-4 MSG

He stooped down. He lowered himself and took on the human condition. He was tempted in all measures like as we are, yet without sin. Let us therefore come boldly unto the throne of grace that we may obtain mercy and find grace to help in time of need. See Hebrews 4. He did not say, come boldly to the throne of judgment. He said, come boldly to the throne of grace. It is there that you will find a faithful high priest that can be touched with the feeling of your infirmities. He was in all points tempted, like as we are, yet without sin. It is there that you will find grace to help. It is there that you learn how to embrace what the spirit is doing in you, instead of redoubling your own efforts. Aren't you glad he stooped down?

- He Wrote in the Sand -

The second thing he does is to write with his finger in the sand. Some say he wrote the names and addresses of all of those who had been to her house. Others say he wrote the secrets of their hearts. I think what was happening is that the finger of the great I Am was touching the sand of her human existence. The human and the divine were finding a connection. It was as if he was taking her all the way back to his original creation in Eden's misty garden when the hand of the creator touched the dust of the earth and formed a man in the image of God. Perhaps he wrote his own name in the sand. Maybe he wrote his signature. If you break the word *signature* down, you might say he *signed his nature*. In the new covenant the goal of the believer should not be just a ticket to heaven when you die. It should be the desire to be conformed to his image and likeness, to bear his nature, to carry his name, to have life through his name. That can only happen as the hand of the great Potter touches the sand of our human existence and forms us into his likeness. Then he breathes into us his very life. It is in that place that he writes his law upon our hearts. Our sins and iniquities he remembers no more.

- He Lifted Up Himself -

As the scribes and Pharisees were screaming, "Moses in the law commanded us that such should be stoned, but what sayest thou"? They were demanding that the law of Moses be fully met. They had the law on their side and justice had to be met. Jesus' response to their accusations was, he lifted up himself. I am reminded of John 12:31-32 where Jesus said, if I be lifted up, I will draw all men unto myself. However, in this text the word men are not in the original Greek text. If you read verse 31, it says, now is the judgment of this world; now shall the Prince of this world be cast out. It was not just all men he drew into himself. It was all judgment. What was taking place with this woman caught in adultery is that Jesus was not circumventing the demand of the law for justice and judgment. When he was lifted up, he drew her judgment into himself. You see, Jesus did not just die for us. He died as us. We were crucified with Christ. We got everything we had coming to us 2000 years ago. Then he said to the multitude, he that is without sin among you, let him first cast a stone at her. When they heard these words, they were convicted by their own conscience and went out one by one. They dropped their rocks and walked away because there was no one in this crowd that could be justified by the works of the law. Jesus was the only one in the crowd without sin. But he had no intention of stoning her.

- Neither Do I Condemn You -

John 8:9 says, and Jesus was left alone, the woman standing in the midst. My question is, if Jesus was all that was left, and the woman was standing in the midst, what was she standing amid? The answer is, she was standing amid *him*. And if you are in him, there is therefore now no condemnation to those who are in Christ Jesus. It is based on truth that we are in him and there is no condemnation. Jesus then said to the woman, where are your accusers? You see, when you are in Christ, it will shut the mouth of the accuser of the brethren because his only weapon is condemnation. When you see your position in Christ and his finished work, then you can declare no weapon formed against you will prosper and any tongue that rises up against you in judgment will be utterly condemned because your righteousness is of me, saith the Lord. Jesus then makes this powerful declaration, "neither do I condemn thee: go, and sin no more." Go and sin no more was not an empty command to bring her back to a performance-based religious system. It was a divine empowerment that would flow from this encounter. What he wrote in the sand of her human existence and the release from condemnation would empower her to walk in the light of life. It is upon the heels of him making this powerful statement that he declares his first "I Am". It is in the very next verse that he says, I am the light of the world: he that follows me shall not walk in darkness but shall have the light of life. What an incredible light had just come into the world. This is a powerful revelation that God did not send his son into the world to condemn the world, but that the world through him might be saved. Whosoever believeth in him should not perish but have the life of the coming age. The light that was piercing the darkness was the revelation that he did not come to condemn us. He came to give us life. God is more interested in healing your brokenness than he is in judging or condemning you. Let us look at this Scripture:

9 And as Jesus passed by, he saw a man which was blind from his birth. 2 And his disciples asked him, saying, Master, who did sin, this man, or his parents, that he was born blind? 3 Jesus answered, Neither hath this man sinned, nor his parents: but that the works of God should be made manifest in him. 4 I must work the works of him that sent me, while it is day: the night cometh, when no man can work. 5 As long as I am in the world, I am the light of the world. John 9:1-5 KJV

In this Scripture the question is, who did sin, this man, or his parents? When you have an old covenant paradigm you are always walking in sin consciousness thinking God is out to get you. You are always looking for someone to blame for the problem. This whole question is absurd to me. If the man were born blind how could he possibly have sinned. Did he sin on the way out of the birth canal? That is how absurd religion can be. The answer Jesus gave them was neither has this man sinned, nor his parents but that the works of God should be manifest in him. In other words, stop the blame game. Stop the sin hunt and realize that God was interested in healing this man's blindness, not in finding someone to judge or condemn. It is upon the heels of this statement that Jesus says, as long as I am in the world, I am the light of the world. It is the light of the glorious gospel that shines in our hearts. This kind of a revelation will make you run *to* God instead of running *from* him.

How we think God treats people determines how we treat them. If we think God is judgmental and angry, that is how we will act. If we have a distorted image of God, we will have a distorted image of humanity. But when we see a God of love, we will walk in love toward his creation. We must return to the water, that is the water of the word; the mirror that

54

contains the image of Abba. For when we look in the mirror we will be changed into the selfsame image from glory to glory. We will receive his unconditional love and then give it away to the next person we meet.

He that saith he is in the light, and hateth his brother, is in darkness even until now. 10 He that loveth his brother abideth in the light, and there is none occasion of stumbling in him. 11 But he that hateth his brother is in darkness, and walketh in darkness, and knoweth not whither he goeth, because that darkness hath blinded his eyes. 12 I write unto you, little children, because your sins are forgiven you for his name's sake. 1 John 2:9-12 KJV

This Scripture makes it abundantly clear that hate is darkness, but whoever loves his brother abides in the light. Jesus was love personified and as such he was the light of the world. Jesus said to his disciples, a new commandment I give unto you, that you love one another, even as I have loved you. For if we walk in the light as he is in the light, we have fellowship with one another and the blood of Jesus Christ his son cleanses us from all sin. In other words, if you love your brother, you are not going to steal from him or take his wife or do him any harm. Love is much stronger than law. It is the love of Christ that constrains us.

Do not think I will accuse you to the father: there is one that accuses you, even Moses, in whom you trust. John 5:45 KJV

Do you see the comparison? Moses and the law were not the light. The old covenant put a vail over our faces. It condemned us. It was exclusive and only included the Jews. Jesus loves, reconciles, and forgives us, and that love, and light is inclusive. It included both Jew and Gentiles. The people in darkness saw a great light. He is the true light. Beloved, let us walk in the light of the great I Am.

- Another Look at the Same Story -

I think it is also possible that the woman caught in adultery is a picture of the adulterous nation of Israel. He was giving them every opportunity to be reconciled to God who was her true husband and apply the blood of the real Lamb to the house of Israel. In the latter part of John eight they rejected the Messiah, which ushered in the inclusion of the Gentiles.

*20 These words spake Jesus in the treasury, as he taught in the temple: and no man laid hands on him; for his hour was not yet come. 21 Then said Jesus again unto them, I go my way, and ye shall seek me, and shall die in your sins: whither I go, ye cannot come. 22 Then said the Jews, Will he kill himself? because he saith, Whither I go, ye cannot come. 23 And he said unto them, Ye are from beneath; I am from above: ye are of this world; I am not of this world. 24 I said therefore unto you, that ye shall die in your sins: **for if ye believe not that I am he, ye shall die in your sins**. John 8:20-24 KJV*

The rulers of the darkness of that age were not just demonic spirits. They were the religious rulers of the day, for they loved darkness more than they loved light. Jesus then begins to define what it means to be the seed of Abraham. The children of Abraham are the children of faith. He tells them if they were the children of Abraham, they would love him and believe his word. But because they sought to kill him for telling them the truth, Jesus declares unto them, you are not Abraham's seed. You are of your father the devil.

*12 For we do not wrestle against flesh and blood, but against principalities, against powers, against the rulers **of the darkness of this age**, against spiritual hosts of wickedness in the heavenly places. Eph. 6:12-13 NKJV*

*39 They answered and said unto him, Abraham is our father. Jesus saith unto them, If ye were Abraham's children, ye would do the works of Abraham. 40 But now ye seek to kill me, a man that hath told you the truth, which I have heard of God: this did not Abraham. 41 Ye do the deeds of your father. Then said they to him, We be not born of fornication; we have one Father, even God. 42 Jesus said unto them, **If God were your Father, ye would love me**: for I proceeded forth and came from God; neither came I of myself, but he sent me. 43 Why do ye not understand my* *speech? even because ye cannot hear my word. 44* **Ye are of your father the devil, and the lusts of your father ye will do.** *He was a murderer from the beginning, and abode not in the truth, because there is no truth in him. When he speaketh a lie, he speaketh of his own: for he is a liar, and the father of it. 45 And because I tell you the truth, ye believe me not. 46 Which of you convinceth me of sin? And if I say the truth, why do ye not believe me? 47 He that is of God heareth God's words: ye therefore hear them not, because ye are not of God. 48 Then answered the Jews, and said unto him, Say we not well that thou art a Samaritan, and hast a devil? 49 Jesus answered, I have not a devil; but I honour my Father, and ye do dishonour me. 50 And I seek not mine own glory: there is one that seeketh and judgeth. 51 Verily, verily, I say unto you, If a man keep my saying, he shall never see death. 52 Then said the Jews unto him, Now we know that thou hast a devil. Abraham is dead, and the prophets; and thou sayest, If a man keep my saying, he shall never taste of death. 53 Art thou greater than our father Abraham, which is dead? and the prophets are dead: whom makest thou thyself? 54 Jesus answered, If I honour myself, my honour is nothing: it is my Father that honoureth me; of whom ye say, that he is your God: 55 Yet ye have not known him; but I know him: and if I should say, I know him not, I shall be a liar like unto you: but I know him, and keep his saying. 56 Your father Abraham rejoiced to see my day: and he saw it, and was glad. 57 Then said the Jews unto him, Thou art not yet fifty years old, and hast thou seen Abraham? 58 Jesus said unto them, Verily, verily, I say unto you,* **Before Abraham was, I am.** John 8:39-58 KJV

The nation of Israel was given every opportunity to receive and believe that Jesus was the Christ, the son of the living God, and that believing they could have life through his name. Many of the signs and miracles throughout the gospel of John should have been powerful signposts to confirm to their hearts that he in fact was the son of the living God. He and the father were one and together they were the great I Am.

Look at what is being declared in the story of Nicodemus. Jesus says to Nicodemus, you must be born again in order to see the kingdom of God. What he is virtually saying to Nicodemus is, your natural genealogy and your natural birth is not enough. You must have a spiritual birth. You must come by faith to be the true children of Abraham. Instead of receiving him, they accused Jesus of being a Samaritan and demon possessed. They were forfeiting their inheritance and the Gentiles were about to be included. The people that sat in darkness were about to see great a light.

I do not think it an accident that immediately following the story of Nicodemus who came to Jesus by night, that a Samaritan woman came to Jesus by day. She was a Gentile. Jesus offered her the water of life. She came to the well of Jacob and she found a well sitting on top of the well. Jesus is truly the well of living water. By the time she was finished with her encounter with Jesus, she became a well. She went into her city and said, come see a man who told me all things I ever did. She recognized that he was Messiah without even seeing a sign. The whole city came out to Jesus and believed because of his words. The Jews sought for a sign and throughout the book of John there is signpost after signpost. Jesus said to the Jews an evil and adulterous generation seek for a sign, but no sign will be given to them, except for the sign of Jonah. The sign of Jonah was a picture of the death, burial, and resurrection of Jesus Christ. Even as Jonah was three days and three nights in the belly of the fish, Jesus was three days and three nights in the heart of the earth.

When the Samaritan woman came to Jesus, she said to him the Jews say we must worship in Jerusalem and our people say we need to worship in this mountain. But Jesus said to her, the hour is coming, and now is when true worshipers will worship him in spirit and in truth. In other words, God is no longer interested in a building or a location in the new covenant. One of the first things that Jesus does in the gospel of John is to go into the temple and cleanse the temple. It is there that he says to them, destroy this temple and in three days I will raise it up again. They thought he was talking about the temple in Jerusalem, but he was talking about the spiritual temple which is his body. He was changing the hermeneutic from a literal interpretation to a spiritual one. What he was saying is you think this is the temple, but that is not the temple. I am the temple of God and we being lively stones are fitly framed together to build a habitation of

God through the spirit. A new living temple was now on the scene and it was not located in one geographical place.

His first sign was at a wedding at Cana. It is at this wedding that Jesus does his first miracle and gives his first sign. Remember, a sign points to something ahead. Perhaps the wedding at Cana was a picture of his own wedding. It was a picture of his new bride. It was a picture of those who enter marriage covenant with him as his bride. In that story Jesus gets six water pots made from stone that were used for the purifying ceremony. Six is the number of man. The water pots made from stone are the earthen vessels of humanity. Jesus was showing them in the new covenant there is a new way to be purified, to fill the earthen vessels of humanity with water. Water and wine are symbolic of the Holy Spirit. In the new covenant we are purified through our union with him in our new marriage covenant. It is there that he fills us with his spirit and purifies us by the inward work of the Holy Spirit. We will explore more signs later in this book. Be assured Jesus was giving the nation of Israel every opportunity to believe and receive and have life through his name. But they continue to be an adulterous woman who would not allow him to stoop down and write his law on their hearts.

- The Water of Jealousy -

Let us look at a passage in the book of Numbers that could possibly fit exactly into the story of the woman caught in adultery. It is the story of the water of jealousy.

12 Speak unto the children of Israel, and say unto them, If any man's wife go aside, and commit a trespass against him, 13 And a man lie with her carnally, and it be hid from the eyes of her husband, and be kept close, and she be defiled, and there be no witness against her, neither she be taken with the manner; 14 And the spirit of jealousy come upon him, and he be jealous of his wife, and she be defiled: or if the spirit of jealousy come upon him, and he be jealous of his wife, and she be not defiled: 15 Then shall the man bring his wife unto the priest, and he shall bring her offering for her, the tenth part of an ephah of barley meal; he shall pour no oil upon it, nor put frankincense thereon; for it is an offering of jealousy, an offering of memorial, bringing iniquity to remembrance 16 And the priest shall bring her near, and set her before the Lord: 17 And the priest shall take holy water in an earthen vessel; and of the dust that is in the floor of the tabernacle the priest shall take, and put it into the water: 18 And the priest shall set the woman before the Lord, and uncover the woman's head, and put the offering of memorial in her hands, which is the jealousy offering: and the priest shall have in his hand the bitter water that causeth the curse: Num. 5:12-18 KJV

In the above story, the accusers brought the alleged adulteress to Jesus. The key to this verse is "she was caught in the very act". Scribes and Pharisees were demanding the death of this woman based on the law. If she really were not "caught in the act" then the situation would default to Numbers five which outlines what to do if someone were suspected of adultery. In the case with the woman in adultery, Jesus calls for the witnesses to come forward by casting the first stones. However, no witnesses come forward. So, for Jesus to completely fulfill the law, he had no choice but to move to the next step which would be the procedures for suspected adultery. This would be the water of jealousy found in Numbers five. Let us look at the procedures.

1. The jealous husband brings his suspected wife to a priest together with the barley offering.

2. The priest escorts the woman to the front of the tabernacle.

3. The priest gives the barley to the woman and uncovers her head.

4. The priest holds the cup containing the mixture of holy water and dust from the floor of the tabernacle and recites an oath in front of the woman.

5. The barley the woman was holding is presented to God as a burnt offering.

6. The woman drinks the mixture now containing the three elements of

60

holy water, dust, and ink.

7. If the woman is guilty her reproductive organs will be rendered useless and her belly will swell, and her thigh will rot, and the woman shall be a curse among the people. If she is innocent, then she shall be free, and shall conceive seed.

What we see in this text is how every element and required ingredient of the law was explained in Numbers five. It was present in the story of the alleged adulteress brought before Jesus in John chapter 8.

They had to bring the suspected adulteress before a high priest. Of course, we know Jesus is our great high priest. The priest would give barley to the woman and we know Jesus was the barley. He was the corn of wheat that fell into the ground and died. He was the fulfillment of the grain offerings of the Old Testament. The next thing was that this event would take place at the temple court using dust from the floor. In John eight they are at the temple and Jesus stoops down and puts his hand in the required holy dust. The element of writing was fulfilled in this text. The next ingredient needed for the water of jealousy would be the holy water. Jesus fully meets this requirement because he was the well of living water. All the ingredients and the requirements were met to fulfill the requirements of the law for the water of jealousy.

However, one thing is missing in this story and that is the jealous husband. Jesus could release this woman from condemnation and free her from the death penalty, even under the law, because ultimately there was no witnesses to testify against her. In this story Israel could be a picture of the adulterous woman, the adulterous wife of Jehovah. Jesus could have been identified as the jealous husband in this story. Instead of accusing her, he releases her by saying, neither do I condemn you, go and sin no more. He was not a jealous husband. He was willing to forgive 70×7. If adulteress Israel continued to live in her whoredoms, even under the law he would be free to give her a writing of divorce and marry another. We see this fulfilled in the book of Revelation when the great harlot finally receives the curses of the law because she refused to repent of her ungodly deeds. She refused to go and sin no more. It was not Jesus who was accusing her or putting a curse on her. It was the law of Moses from which she refused to be free. Remember in the above Scripture Jesus said, there is one that accuses you, even Moses, but do not think I will accuse you to the Father. He was giving the adulterous nation of Israel every opportunity to come back to the wedding feast and drink the new wine of the new covenant and not the curse of the water of jealousy. But in the book of Revelation she chooses to drink the cursed cup. All she would have to do is believe and receive according to the procedure in Numbers. This would also make the man guiltless from iniquity and the woman would have to bear her own iniquity. Our husband Jesus fulfilled all the requirements of the law so he could be considered guiltless.

29 This is the law of jealousies, when a wife goeth aside to another instead of her husband, and is defiled; 30 Or when the spirit of jealousy cometh upon him, and he be jealous over his wife, and shall set the woman before the Lord, and the priest shall execute upon her all this law. 31 **Then shall the man be guiltless from iniquity, and this woman shall bear her iniquity.** *Num. 5:29-31 KJV*

Moses and his law were not the true light. Jesus said, "I Am the light of the world, you search the Scriptures and in them you think you have eternal life, but they are they which testify of me. You will not come to me, that you might have life." The Scriptures that he was talking about were the Old Testament Scriptures. The life of the coming age was being offered to them if they would have only understood that all the Scriptures pointed to him.

In the Old Testament, it was Jesus concealed. In the New Testament, it is Jesus revealed. In the Old Testament, it is the shadow. In the New Testament, we live in the substance. In the volume of the book, it was written about him: A Revelation of this kind of light will surely give you the abundant life.

CHAPTER 4
I AM THE BREAD OF LIFE

6 After these things Jesus went over the sea of Galilee, which is the sea of Tiberias. 2 And a great multitude followed him, because they saw his miracles which he did on them that were diseased. 3 And Jesus went up into a mountain, and there he sat with his disciples. 4 And the passover, a feast of the Jews, was nigh. 5 When Jesus then lifted up his eyes, and saw a great company come unto him, he saith unto Philip, Whence shall we buy bread, that these may eat? 6 And this he said to prove him: for he himself knew what he would do. John 6:1-6 KJV

Let me set the stage for the context of the next time Jesus said, "I am the bread of life". Jesus had just crossed over the sea and a great multitude followed him because they saw his miracles. It is following the feast of Passover. They are now in the wilderness and a great company come to him. Does that remind you of any of the stories in the Bible? This miracle should have taken the mind of the first-century Israelite back to the Exodus story. It should have made them remember that the children of Israel left Egypt after the Passover and they also crossed the sea. They came to a wilderness and were hungry for bread and God gave them manna to eat. Here we are with an almost exact replica of the first Exodus. Except this time the leader of the real Exodus, Jesus Christ, has now led them across the sea and into the wilderness after the Passover.

When Jesus saw such a great multitude he said to Philip, go buy bread that these may eat. He said this to prove Philip because he already knew what he would do. The reason he knew what he would do is because this is not the first time the great I Am ever fed a multitude in the wilderness. He knew he was going to give them the true bread from heaven.

One of his disciples named Andrew said to him, there is a lad here that has five barley loaves and two small fish but what are they among so many? I think this young lad represents the next generation of Israelites who would be the one to go into the promise land. The older generation was about to die in the wilderness again because of unbelief. Remember, in the Exodus journey, they died because of their unbelief. They believed the negative report of the 10 spies.

Joshua and Caleb, however, had a different report. Now one greater than Joshua is on the scene. It is not an accident that the name Joshua is the Hebrew name for Jesus. The generation that Jesus spoke of in Matthew chapters 23-24 that were alive during this 40-year transition period from 30 A.D. to 70 A.D., were the generation that did not believe the report of the Lord. They were the terminal generation that would die in the wilderness.

- The Book of Hebrews: A Book of Better Things -

The entire book of Hebrews is written to literal first-century Hebrews. The word Hebrews itself comes from are word that means *to cross over*. But this time they were not crossing over out of a physical bondage. They were crossing over out of a spiritual bondage. They were coming out of the religious bondage of an old covenant paradigm. They were leaving the Egypt of spiritual bondage. The book of Hebrews is an incredible treaty of new covenant truth. It is a book that was written to Hebrews to show them what was better about the new covenant than the old covenant.

In Hebrews chapter 1 Jesus is better than the prophets because God has in these last days spoken to us by his Son. The last days he was talking about in this text is not the last days of this age. It was the last days of the old covenant age. In Hebrews chapter 1 Jesus is better than Angels.

In Hebrews chapter 2 the reason he is better than Angels is because the first covenant was given by the hand of Angels. The new covenant was given by a Son who would be the heir of all things. He took not on him the nature of Angels, but he took on him the seed of Abraham.

In Hebrews chapter 3 Jesus is better than Moses because Moses was a servant in the house. But Christ is son over his own house; whose house we are.

In Hebrews chapter 4 rest in the finished work of Jesus Christ is a better promise land. He tells them in Hebrews chapter 4 that the first generation under Moses did not enter the promise land of rest because of unbelief. That is exactly what Jesus was addressing to this multitude in the wilderness in John's gospel, their unbelief.

In Hebrews chapter 5 he has a better priesthood. He is better than Levi. He is a priest forever after the order of Melchisedec, and as such he serves bread and wine. That is his finished work. He is a faithful high priest who can be touched with the feelings of our infirmities so that we can come boldly to the throne of grace and obtain mercy and find grace to help the time of need.

In Hebrews chapter 6 he warns them not to go back to Judaism once they had tasted the powers of the age to come. The coming age was the new covenant age. He warned them not to fall away and return to animal sacrifice, because if they did, they would crucify to themselves the Son of God afresh and put him to an open shame. Such actions would say that the blood of Jesus is not enough and it would do despite, to the spirit of grace. Hebrews chapter 10 repeats this same warning. He tells them if they sin willfully after they received the knowledge of the truth, there would remain no more sacrifice for sin. The word sin in this text does not mean what you did Saturday night. It means to miss the mark. The mark they were missing was failing to hold fast the profession of their faith without wavering. They were going back to animal sacrifice because of the pressures and persecution that they were experiencing in this 40-year transition period when the law was fading away. They were suffering the spoiling of their goods and the loss of loved ones in the arenas, etc. When he tells them there remains no more offering for sin, he is not saying you cannot be forgiven for what you did on Saturday night even if you did it on purpose. He is saying, if you go back to animal sacrifice and the blood of bulls and goats, there is not another sin offering coming. Then he warns them of a fiery indignation and a judgment that was coming. That judgment came in 70 A.D. at the dismantling of this whole system of

65

sacrifice.

In Hebrews chapter 7 there is a better priesthood, and since there is a change of priesthood there must be a change of the law. The priesthood of Levi is made after the law of carnal commandment. But the new covenant priesthood of Melchisedec is made after the power of an endless life. It is in that same chapter Jesus is made a surety of a better testament.

In Hebrews chapter 8 it speaks of a better sanctuary and a better tabernacle. There are better gifts and sacrifices. There is a more excellent ministry. There is the mediator of a better covenant established on better promises. God finds fault with the first covenant and declares, behold, the days are coming when I will make a new covenant with the house of Israel and the house of Judah. In this new covenant he will write his laws upon our hearts and upon our minds. He will be merciful to our unrighteousness and our sins, and iniquities he will remember no more. The fact that he declared a new covenant has made the first one old, and now that which is decaying and waxes old is about to vanish away.

In Hebrews chapter 9 there is a better tabernacle and a better sanctuary. There is a better mediator of a better covenant. There is a better entrance into the most holy place by the blood of Jesus.

In Hebrews chapter 10 he declares that the law was only a shadow of good things to come. He also declares that there are better sacrifices than the blood of bulls and goats. Sanctification and perfection are not based on your performance but on the perfect sacrifice that Jesus offered once for all. He then warns them again, do not sin willfully and go back to Judaism. Do not repudiate the blood of this covenant. Do not do so despite to the spirit of grace. He tells them in this chapter, now the just will live by faith, but if any man draws back, my soul shall have no pleasure in him. We are not of them who draw back unto perdition, but of them that believe to the saving of the soul. In other words, do not go back. Remember Lot's wife? There is nothing to go back to. That was the warning he gave them in Matthew chapter 24 when he told them, when you see Jerusalem compassed with armies, flee into the mountains. In other words, there is nothing in Judaism worth going back to. Judgment was coming upon that system and that city. Just like Sodom and Gomorrah, fire was about to rain down on Jerusalem and the elements were about to melt with fervent heat. That was the perdition and judgment. This is what he was warning them about in this chapter when he said, *"But a certain fearful looking for a fiery indignation."* Heb. 10:27 This is exactly what happened in A.D. 70.

In Hebrews chapter 11 he points them to their heroes of faith. All these men did something in the visible realm that was a picture of the redemptive work of Christ. Abraham offered up Isaac. That is a picture of God offering up his only begotten Son. Moses keeps the Passover. That is a picture of the true Lamb of God bringing us out of Egypt. These men did something in the visible realm that was a picture of the redemptive work of Jesus Christ. The latter part of Hebrews 11 says these all died in faith, not receiving the promise because God had some better thing in store for us. The better thing was the new covenant. Now faith is a substance. In other words, I am not believing because I think God is going to do something. I am believing because he already has. The substance was the finished work of Jesus Christ.

In Hebrews chapter 12 he opens by saying, lay aside every weight and the sin that does so easily beset you and run with patience the race set before you looking unto Jesus, who is the author and finisher of our faith. In other words, take your focus off your Old Testament heroes and put your focus on the person and work of Jesus Christ. The weight and the sin that besets us in the context of this book is not what you did Saturday night. It is trying to carry the weight of an old covenant performance system and it is missing the mark, sinning by going back to Judaism. It is why in this same chapter that he tells them to lift the hands that hang down and strengthen the feeble knees. I am afraid so many people are worn out and tired because of a performance- based religious system that has no supply. Then he warns them not to be like Esau who sold his birthright for one morsel of meat. That is exactly what was happening with this terminal generation that Jesus was dealing with in the first century. They were about to sell their birthright and lose the inheritance by going back to Judaism, selling their birthright for one morsel of meat. It is in that same chapter that he declares to them, for you did not come to blackness and darkness. You did not come to a God who said, stay away or you will be thrust through with a dart. That mountain was Mount Sinai and he told them plainly, you have not come to this mountain. But that is the mountain we bring people to every Sunday in our churches. He goes on to say, but you are come to Mount Zion. You have already come to the city of the living God and to the heavenly Jerusalem. Zion represents the new covenant, while Sinai represents the old covenant. You see an old covenant, and an old city of Jerusalem was about to pass off the scene. A new Jerusalem, the bride, the Lamb's wife was coming on the scene. In Hebrews chapter 12 he tells them clearly that Jesus is the mediator of a new covenant and that there is better blood than the blood of Abel. Abel's blood cries for vengeance, while the blood of Jesus says, Father, forgive them for they know not what they do.

Then he warns them again, do not refuse him who is speaking to you from heaven. He warns of a coming shaking and that everything that can be shaken will be shaken. That text is not talking about a coming shaking. It is not about pandemics, nuclear wars, or political upheaval in our future. It is talking about the shaking of this old covenant system. The removal of old Jerusalem with all its trappings and what would remain, would be a kingdom that cannot be shaken or moved. It is in that context that he said, let us have grace whereby we may serve God acceptably with reverence and godly fear.

In Hebrews 13, he concludes by talking about behavior under the new covenant. Then he states, the reason this book was written is so that your heart could be established in grace.

Yes, the generation Jesus was talking to in the first century, many of them would die in the wilderness. But be encouraged, this next generation was carrying bread and fish. Bread and fish were the meal that Jesus offered his disciples after his resurrection, after they had toiled all night and caught no fish. When they came to the shore, they found Jesus with bread and fish on the fire. I think one of the reasons that they toiled all night is because they were fishing on the wrong side of the ship. They were fishing on the old covenant side of the ship. The old covenant side of the ship is full of toil, labor, and work. But if you cast your net on the other side of the ship, that is the new covenant side. You will bring in a great multitude of fish. We must use a different kind of bait if are going to bring in a multitude of fish. We cannot keep fishing with the same old covenant bait and hope to catch fish. The old covenant bait was nothing but fear, manipulation, and threats. All we did was scare the fish away. Jesus came to offer a different kind of meal. He had bread and fish on the fire. The fact that there were five loaves carries with it the idea of the message of grace. The biblical number five means grace. Two was the number of union and unity in the Scripture. The fish was also the symbol used by the first-century believers that they were followers of Christ. Perhaps what is being pictured here is Jesus is offering grace and union with him as the new diet for the multitude.

I believe we are living in a season where there is a great reformation and the next generation is carrying something that we must recognize. We must not marginalize or underestimate the value of those who are coming on the scene in this hour that are much younger than we. They are carrying something that we may need. And they may very well be the generation that will see the fullness of living in this promise land called rest. They are anxious, ready, and excited to carry a message of grace and union. However, we must mention the fact that someone had to pack this young lad's lunch. While we honor and value the next generation, we must not forget that there are mothers, grandmothers, Joshuas and Calebs that have preceded this generation and imparted unto them what they now carry. We must give honor where honor is due.

- Green Pastures -

The next thing Jesus says is, "Make the men sit down." Now there was much grass in the place. About 5000 men sat down. In Mark 6:39, it is his version of the same story, except he points out that he commanded them to sit down by companies upon the *green* grass. I think it is important that he mentions *green* grass. The reason being that in Psalm chapter 23, the Lord is my shepherd he makes me lie down in *green* pastures. I will have more to say about this in the chapter "I am the good Shepherd". But I must mention here that the Lord is your shepherd and he will always bring you to a place of rest where you can lie down in green pastures. It is the place he restores your soul.

In Revelation chapter 4 of the heavenly vision of the throne, John the revelator declares, I saw a rainbow around about the throne in sight like unto an emerald. The rainbow is a symbol of the covenant God made with Noah. It is round about the throne in this same chapter. The throne represents the kingdom and the rainbow represents the covenant in which the kingdom operates: the new covenant. It is the color of an emerald which is green. Green symbolizes the new covenant.

In Song of Solomon the bride declares, "behold our bed is green". The bed symbolizes the place of rest and the place of reproduction.

In Psalm 92:10 the psalmist declares, "I shall be anointed with fresh oil". The Hebrew word for fresh in this text literally means *green*. The psalmist is saying, I will be anointed with green oil. What that says to me is that there was a fresh anointing that was coming. That anointing was a new covenant anointing. Oh, that God would anoint his ministers today with the green anointing of new covenant truth. Only then as under-shepherds will we be able to bring God's people to rest in green pastures. It is only then that we will be able to bring them into the very throne room of God with its green rainbow. Only then will his bride be able to find rest and declare our bed is green. Surely the Lord is my shepherd. He makes me lie down in green pastures.

- He Distributes it to His Disciples -

The next thing he does is gives thanks, break the bread, and distributed to his disciples. When the multitude was all filled, he told his disciples to gather up the fragments that remain. Nothing will be lost. They took up

12 baskets full of fragments, five barley loaves and two small fish. This is an incredible picture of kingdom distribution. This was pointing to the fact that Jesus Christ is the true bread from heaven, and he was going to be broken and given as the final Passover Lamb. The night before his decease, in an upper room, he took the bread and blessed it and said, this is my body which is broken for you, take and eat. This was the covenant meal.

What he was saying to his disciples was, this is the last lamb you will ever have to kill because the real Lamb of God was about to be sacrificed. When we feed on the bread, we are feeding on his finished work. He said to them in the upper room, as often as you come together, do this to remember me. You could find in the word *remember* the idea of put me back together again. *RE*-member me. He uses the same word in the great communion text in Corinthians. When they came together to eat the covenant meal, they did it in remembrance of him. It was a symbol that they were part of the body of Christ, and as such, they being many were one bread.

They were the carriers of the bread of heaven, and they were called to distribute the message of his finished work. They were called to be priests after the order of Melchisedec, who brought forth bread and wine which symbolized the finished work of Jesus Christ. I would ask you today, what are you serving? What are you distributing to the world? Are you a Levitical priest serving up the old covenant of death or are you a new covenant priest serving bread and wine?

It is not an accident that they took up 12 baskets full. There were 12 apostles and these 12 apostles would carry the message of the finished work to the nations of the earth. In the old covenant it was established upon 12 tribes. In the new covenant it is established through 12 apostles.

Jesus tells his apostles to get in the ship and go to the other side. They were headed to the other side all right. They were headed to the new covenant side. They were to carry the message of his finished work from the old covenant age into the full manifestation of the new covenant age.

71

What they did not know was that great opposition awaited them, tumultuous winds, stormy seas, darkness and being tossed about. All of this was a description of the things that they would suffer in the next 40 years in order to carry the message of the new covenant. It was amid just such a storm that Jesus came walking on the water. Jesus was demonstrating to them that walking on the water was a symbol of walking in the spirit and walking by faith. Sometimes you need faith to get out of the ship and abandon the safety of the old covenant ship. By faith, learn to walk on water. Sometimes you need to know when it is time to abandon ship like the apostle Paul did on his way to Rome. He said to his colleagues, I perceive that this journey is with much hurt. They lost the ship. It broke apart, but not a life was lost.

Ministries today hesitate to preach the Gospel, because they are afraid it will break up the ship. It may break up their *fellow – ship* or make their church smaller. Some have already experienced the loss of their ship. They are swimming to shore holding onto the pieces of the ship that still float. It is in this season that we are learning what to let go of and want to hold onto. It was after this experience on the island of Melita that the apostle Paul shook the serpent off his hand and was not affected by the poison. The same people who accused him, incarcerated him, and called him a murderer or something worse, are now saying he is a god.

If you are moved by the crowd, you will find that one minute they love you and the next minute they hate you. What you must decide is, do I want the favor of God or do I want the favor of men. I say to you, shake off the snake. You must still carry your message to Rome.

Sometimes you must invite Jesus onto the ship. How quickly even the apostles forgot the miracle of the loaves and fish. In the moments when the ship was tossed, they should have defaulted to the last miracle that Jesus did, the miracle of the loaves and fish. There was a basket for each one of the 12 apostles. He warned them later to beware of the leaven of the Pharisees. In that context he says to them, do you not remember the miracle of the loaves and the fish and how many baskets were collected? They replied, 12. It should have dawned on them that there was a basket for each one of them. How quickly we forget the last miracle God did for us. I want to encourage leaders that if you are going through tumultuous winds to preach this new covenant, remember you are carrying a basket full of the miraculous. You are carrying a basket full of the finished work of Jesus Christ. You are not a basket case. You will get to the other side. Take heart. Jesus is in the ship with you.

- The Bread of Life -

*25 And when they had found him on the other side of the sea, they said unto him, Rabbi, when camest thou hither? 26 Jesus answered them and said, Verily, verily, I say unto you, Ye seek me, not because ye saw the miracles, but because ye did eat of the loaves, and were filled. 27 Labour not for the meat which perisheth, but for that meat which endureth unto everlasting life, which the Son of man shall give unto you: for him hath God the Father sealed. 28 Then said they unto him, What shall we do, that we might work the works of God? 29 Jesus answered and said unto them, **This is the work of God, that ye believe on him whom he hath sent**. 30 They said therefore unto him, **What sign shewest thou then**, that we may see, and believe thee? what dost thou work? 31 Our fathers did eat manna in the desert; as it is written, He gave them bread from heaven to eat. 32 Then Jesus said unto them, Verily, verily, I say unto you, **Moses gave you not that bread from heaven;** but my Father giveth you the true bread from heaven. 33 For the bread of God is he which cometh down from heaven, and giveth life unto the world. 34 Then said they unto him, Lord, evermore give us this bread. 35 And Jesus said unto them, **I am the bread of life:** he that cometh to me shall never hunger; and he that believeth on me shall never thirst. 36 But I said unto you, That ye also have seen me, and believe not. John 6:25-36 KJV*

Following such an incredible miracle, these people had the audacity to ask him, what sign do you show us that we can see and believe. Jesus just performed one of the most incredible miracles they had probably ever seen. It was an exact replica of the Exodus journey when God gave them manna from heaven. Then he gave them an incredible sign. I think he

73

probably looked at them and thought, what more I could show you. You are just like the children of Israel in the wilderness. You see miracle after miracle and still you do not believe. Jesus said to them, "labor not for the meat which perishes, but for that meat which endures unto everlasting life." He was offering them the life of the coming age, but all they could think about was natural bread. They did exactly what the children of Israel did in the wilderness under the leadership of Moses. They murmured among themselves. See John 6:43.

*6 Now these things were our examples, to the intent we should not lust after evil things, as they also lusted. 7 Neither be ye idolaters, as were some of them; as it is written, The people sat down to eat and drink, and rose up to play. 8 Neither let us commit fornication, as some of them committed, and fell in one day three and twenty thousand. 9 Neither let us tempt Christ, as some of them also tempted, and were destroyed of serpents. 10 **Neither murmur ye, as some of them also murmured**, and were destroyed of the destroyer. 11 Now all these things happened unto them for ensamples: and they are written for our admonition, upon whom the ends of the world are come. 1 Cor. 10:6-11 KJV*

They asked Jesus, what must we do to work the works of God? He replied, "This is the work of God, that you believe on him whom he hath sent". The work of God in the new covenant is to simply believe and you will have life through his name. All these signs were given that you might believe that Jesus is the Christ. But they kept missing the signs. It is in this context that Jesus says to them, Moses gave you bread from heaven, but my Father gives you the *true* bread from heaven. In other words, you thought that was the bread, but that was not *the* bread. I Am the true bread that came down from heaven.

*41 The **Jews then murmured** at him, because he said, **I am the bread** which came down from heaven. 42 And they said, Is not this Jesus, the son of Joseph, whose father and mother we know? how is it then that he saith, I came down from heaven? 43 Jesus therefore answered and said unto them, **Murmur not among yourselves**. 44 No man can come to me, except the Father which hath sent me draw him: and I will raise him up at the last* day. *45 It is written in the prophets, And they shall be all taught of God. Every man therefore that hath heard, and hath learned of the Father, cometh unto me. 46 Not that any man hath seen the Father, save he which is of God, he hath seen the Father. 47 Verily, verily, I say unto you, He that believeth on me **hath everlasting life.** 48 **I am that bread of life.** 49 Your fathers did eat manna in the wilderness, and are dead. 50 This is the bread which cometh down from heaven, that a man may eat thereof, and not die. 51 I am the living bread which came down from heaven: if any man eat of this bread, he shall live for ever: **and the bread that I will give is my flesh, which I will give for the life of the world.** 52 The Jews therefore strove among themselves, saying, How can this man give us his flesh to eat? 53 Then Jesus said unto them, Verily, verily, I say unto you, **Except ye eat the flesh of the Son of man, and drink his blood, ye have no life in you.** 54 **Whoso eateth my flesh, and drinketh my blood, hath eternal life; and I will raise him up at the last day.** 55 For my flesh is meat indeed, and my blood is drink indeed. 56 He that eateth my flesh, and drinketh my blood, dwelleth in me, and I in him. 57 As the living Father hath sent me, and I live by the Father: so he that eateth me, even he shall live by me. 58 This is that bread which came down from heaven: not as your fathers did eat manna and are dead: he that eateth of this bread shall live for ever.* John 6:41-58 KJV

The Jews and many of his followers were offended by his sayings. They could not understand the spiritual implications. In the mind of the first-century Jew, they would have remembered the law of Moses that said, you are not supposed to eat anything that has blood. Many of his followers left him after he said these things.

Can you imagine having 5000 men in church this Sunday, not counting women and children? Then you preach a message and all of them leave you. Even the 12 were not too sure of him. But he was teaching them a new way of thinking. He was not talking about natural blood and natural flesh. He was talking about his death, burial, and resurrection. The covenant meal of communion would represent that very thing the night before his decease. When we feed on his finished work, we are eating his

75

flesh and drinking his blood. I say, Lord, evermore give us this bread.

CHAPTER 5
I AM THE DOOR

10 Verily, verily, I say unto you, He that entereth not by the door into the sheepfold, but climbeth up some other way, the same is a thief and a robber. 2 But he that entereth in by the door is the shepherd of the sheep. 3 To him the porter openeth; and the sheep hear his voice: and he calleth his own sheep by name, and leadeth them out.

4 And when he putteth forth his own sheep, he goeth before them, and the sheep follow him: for they know his voice. 5 And a stranger will they not follow, but will flee from him: for they know not the voice of strangers. 6 This parable spake Jesus unto them: but they understood not what things they were which he spake unto them. 7 Then said Jesus unto them again, Verily, verily, I say unto you, I am the door of the sheep. 8 All that ever came before me are thieves and robbers: but the sheep did not hear them. 9 I am the door: by me if any man enter in, he shall be saved, and shall go in and out, and find pasture. 10 The thief cometh not, but for to steal, and to kill, and to destroy: I am come that they might have life, and that they might have it more abundantly. John 10:1-10 KJV

Let me draw your attention to the first verse. He is telling them, if you think there is some other way into the sheepfold than through the door, the same will become a thief and a robber to you. Remember, in the previous chapters I wrote concerning the seven times Jesus said, "I Am", he always says it in contrast to something from the old covenant. In other words, you thought the law of Moses was the light, but that is not the light. I am the light. You thought the bread that Moses gave you was the true bread, but that is not the true bread. I am the true bread that came down from heaven. You thought the natural building was the temple, but that is not the temple I am the temple of the living God. In this chapter I want to draw your attention to what they thought was the door into life. The door that they thought would lead them into life was performance-based Christianity through old covenant works and labor. However, that system would prove to be a thief to them. It was the way that "seems right" to a man. The end thereof is always death. Notice, it does not say there is a way that seems wrong to a man, but there is a way that seems right to him, Proverbs 14:12. I submit to you the idea that they thought the way into life was through the law of Moses and the keeping of rules, except it did not give them life. It took their life. It became a thief unto them. In other words, they thought that Moses and his law was the door into life, but what Jesus was saying is, " That is not the door, I am the door."

*13 Enter ye in at the strait gate: for wide is the gate, and broad is the way, that leadeth to destruction, and many there be which go in thereat: 14 Because strait is the gate, and narrow is the way, **which leadeth unto life**, and few there be that find it.* Matt. 7:13-14 KJV

Let us compare this verse with Luke's version of the same story.

24 Strive to enter in at the strait gate: for many, I say unto you, will seek to enter in, and shall not be able. 25 When once the master of the house is risen up, and hath shut to the door, and ye begin to stand without, and to knock at the door, saying, Lord, Lord, open unto us; and he shall answer and say unto you, I know you not whence ye are: 26 Then shall ye begin to say, We have eaten and drunk in thy presence, and thou hast taught in our streets. 27 But he shall say, I tell you, I know you not whence ye are; depart from me, all ye workers of iniquity. 28 There shall be weeping and gnashing of teeth, when ye shall see Abraham, and Isaac, and Jacob, and all the prophets, in the kingdom of God, and you yourselves thrust out. 29 And they shall come from the east, and from the west, and from the north, and from the south, and shall sit down in the kingdom of God. 30 And, behold, there are last which shall be first, and there are first which shall be last. Luke 13:24-30 KJV

Have you ever heard someone say to you, I just need to get back on the straight and narrow, or when I get my act together, I am going to go back to church? I reply, if you get your act together, it is just an act. God is not interested in actors. As a matter of fact, the word hypocrite means an actor on the stage of life.

I have added the text from Matthew's gospel because it describes the result of being on the straight and narrow. The first thing I want to point out in this text is that the strait gate and the narrow way does not lead to heaven. It leads to life. Often, we read into the text something that is not there. This text is not talking about you making it to heaven. He is talking about you entering life in the kingdom right now. If you enter now, heaven is included in the package. Remember that this book is about believing and having a life through his name; the life of the coming age which is life in the new covenant.

- The Thief of John 10 is Not the Devil -

All that ever came before him were thieves and robbers. Notice, he said "ALL" that ever came before me. What came before him was Moses and the law and it did not produce life. It produced death. That is why it is called the law of sin and death and that is why Jesus had to come and die. It was to meet the demands of a system that required death. His resurrection afforded us entrance into life. Most people preach that the thief of John 10:10 is the devil. However, the devil is not mentioned in this text. The thief of John 10 is not the devil. The thief of John 10 is some other way. When you think there is some other way, it will become a thief and a robber to you. When you think you can enter in through your own human effort and through religious observances, it will take your life and give you a horribly skewed world view. You will become so miserable that all you can do is long for heaven. You will sing songs like One More Valley and One More Hill, It'll All Be Over After a While, Just a Few More Weary Days and Then, In the Sweet By and By, etc. This is because you have missed the point of the abundant life, living as a citizen in the kingdom. I believe one day I will stand before God and he will high-five me and say I had a hoot living in your body, wasn't that an exciting journey! It was the days of heaven on earth. It was life in the promise land; a land that flowing with milk and honey.

I heard someone say once if you play country music backwards you get your truck back. You get out of jail. You will not get run over with the train and your wife will come back. But I sometimes think if we play gospel music backwards, we will get our life back. We would get our peace, joy and looks back. Our kids would come back. We would get our money back, etc. After all, salvation is much bigger than just a ticket to heaven. It is him saving us spirit, soul, and body.

- The Fig Tree -

I added the text from Luke's gospel above so that you could see the context of what Jesus was speaking. The few verses here talk about the fig tree.

6 He spake also this parable; A certain man had a fig tree planted in his vineyard; and he came and sought fruit thereon, and found none. 7 Then said he unto the dresser of his vineyard, Behold, these three years I come seeking fruit on this fig tree, and find none: cut it down; why cumbereth it the ground? 8 And he answering said unto him, Lord, let it alone this year also, till I shall dig about it, and dung it: 9 And if it bear fruit, well: and if not, then after that thou shalt cut it down. Luke 13:6-9 KJV

The first point I want to make is that the fig tree is where Adam got the leaves to cover his nakedness in the garden of Eden. It was man's attempt to cover his nakedness once he had eaten from the tree of the knowledge of good and evil. It was man's attempt at self-righteousness. However, God gave them coats of skin. I have many things I could say about this but suffice to say that it could be possible that God had to kill an animal in order to give them a coat of skin. This could point us to the greater fulfillment in the New Testament where we are clothed with the righteousness of God because of the death of the Lamb Christ Jesus. My point here is that Jesus cursed the fig tree because it did not produce fruit. Man's self-righteous efforts through the law can never take away his shame. It can never produce life. It will always leave you in lack and falling short.

The second thing I want to say about this is that natural Israel is pictured throughout the Scriptures as the fig tree. It was the nation that Jesus was talking about in this parable. They were the fig tree that was planted in his vineyard, except they were not producing fruit through their old covenant system. In the parable Jesus says, a certain man had a fig tree planted in his vineyard and he came and sought fruit thereon and found none. Then he said unto the dressers of his vineyard, behold, these three years I came seeking fruit on this fig tree and found none. Cut it down. Why cumbereth it the ground. The dresser of the vineyard would have been natural Israel. Jesus came with a 3 ½-year ministry and for the first three years of his ministry he sought fruit on this fig tree and found none. He told them to let it alone this year also until I dig about it and fertilize it. If it bears fruit, okay. If not, then it will be cut down. That fig tree did not produce any fruit, so it was about to be hewn down and cast into the fire. But let us look at the story of the fig tree in Matthew's gospel.

*19 And when he saw a fig tree in the way, he came to it, **and found nothing thereon, but leaves only, and said unto it, Let no fruit grow on thee henceforward for ever.** And presently the fig tree withered away. 20 And when the disciples saw it, they marvelled, saying, How soon is the fig tree withered away! 21 Jesus answered and said unto them, Verily I say unto you, **If ye have faith, and doubt not, ye shall not only do this which is done to the fig tree, but also if ye shall say unto this mountain, Be thou removed, and be thou cast into the sea; it shall be done.** Matt. 21:19-21 KJV*

This fig leaf religion had no fruit on it. The first message of John the Baptist to the nation of Israel was repent, the kingdom of heaven is at hand and bring forth therefore fruit for repentance. He went on to say, now the ax is laid to the root of the tree and every tree that does not bring forth good fruit is hewn down and cast into the fire. See Matthew chapter 3. The ax was about to be laid to the root of this tree and this nation was about to lose its inheritance. If you look at the above text in Luke, he tells them that once the master of the house is risen and has shut the door, they will begin to stand outside and knock on the door. They will say, Lord, Lord, open to us. He will then answer, I know you not. Jesus is the master of the house and he is the only door. If you reject that door, there is no other way into life. Then they will stand outside and say to him, we have eaten and drunk in your presence and you have taught in our streets. It puts the context of this message in the first century to the Pharisees and the religious rulers of the day because they were the ones that heard him preach in their streets. They were the ones that ate and drank in his presence. But he will say to them, depart from me all you workers of iniquity. I do not know you. Then there will be weeping and gnashing of teeth when they see Abraham, Isaac, and Jacob and all the prophets of the kingdom of God. But they themselves will be cast out.

Then he talks about the inclusion of the Gentiles when he says to them, they will come from the east, from the West, from the North and from the South. They shall sit down in the kingdom of God and behold, there are last which shall be first and there are first which shall be last. What he is saying is that they that were first was the nation of Israel. They had the opportunity to enter the strait gate that leads to life and rejected it. Now they are about to become the last. The Gentiles, which were the last, are now about to become the first because they are entering into the correct door that is Jesus Christ. He is the door into the sheepfold and if you climb up some other way, the same is as a thief and a robber. Please understand that I am not anti-Semitic. I do not hate Jews. I am just pro-Jesus and I am saying God loves both Jew and Gentile. He is including all men. There is no other name given under heaven whereby men must be saved, except the name of Jesus.

As he taught the message about the fig tree in the gospel of Matthew, he said to them, if you have faith and doubt not, you will not only do this which is done to the fig tree. If you will say unto this mountain, be thou removed and cast into the sea, it will be done. Jesus then began to introduce the concept of faith. Faith is the currency of the new covenant. Remember the point of this whole book is these things are written that you might believe that Jesus is the Christ, and that believing you would have life through his name. It is by faith and believing in him that this incredible life flows. He then says to them, if you have faith as a grain of mustard seed, you will say to this mountain, be removed and be cast into the sea.

In this verse Jesus mentioned the mustard seed and he said the kingdom of God is like a grain of mustard seed. In other words, if you have faith, kingdom faith, then you have mountain-moving faith. This faith can move the mountains in your life, but something much bigger than the mountain in your life is being declared here. In Revelation 8:8 it says, the second Angel sounded and as it were a great mountain burning with fire, was cast into the sea. I submit to you the possibility that this mountain that is being removed and cast into the sea is Mount Sinai. It is the mountain in Hebrews chapter 12 that burned with fire and it was full of blackness, darkness, fear, and trembling. If you touched the edge of the mountain, you would be thrust through with a dart. It was on the mountain that Moses said, I exceedingly fear and quake. It was Mount Sinai where the law was given. But if you have faith as a grain of a mustard seed, if you have kingdom faith; then this mountain has been removed and cast into the sea and has been replaced with Mount Zion which symbolizes the new covenant in Hebrews chapter 12. If you have faith and doubt not, you can say to this mountain of legalism in your life, be removed and cast into the sea. In Zachariah, the mountain is removed by shouting grace, grace. Compare these two Scriptures.

*6 Then he answered and spake unto me, saying, This is the word of the Lord unto Zerubbabel, saying, **Not by might, nor by power, but by my spirit, saith the Lord of hosts**. 7 Who art thou, O great mountain? before Zerubbabel thou shalt become a plain: and he shall bring forth the headstone thereof with shoutings, crying, **Grace, grace unto it**. Zech. 4:6-7 KJV*

*16 And of his fulness have all we received, **and grace for grace**. 17 For the law was given by Moses, but grace and truth came by Jesus Christ. John 1:16-17 KJV*

That my friend is truly mountain-moving faith. But it is moving a specific mountain, Mount Sinai, the mountain where the law was given according to Galatians chapter 3. The apostle Paul said that when the law is preached it shuts up faith. For the law is not of faith.

*8 And the scripture, foreseeing that God **would justify the heathen through faith**, preached before the gospel unto Abraham, saying, In thee shall all nations be blessed.*

*9 So then they which be of faith are blessed with faithful Abraham. 10 **For as many as are of the works of the law are under the curse**: for it is written, Cursed is every one that continueth not in all things which are written in the book of the law to do them. 11 But that no man is justified by the law in the sight of God, it is evident: for, The just shall live by faith. 12 **And the law is not of faith**: but, The man that doeth them shall live in them. 13 Christ hath redeemed us from the curse of the law, being made a curse for us: for it is written, Cursed is every one that hangeth on a tree: 14 That the blessing of Abraham might come on the Gentiles through Jesus Christ; that we might receive the promise of the Spirit through faith.* Gal. 3:8-14 KJV

- The Law Shuts Up Faith -

In Hebrews chapter 11, the great hall of faith, it talks about Moses who chose to suffer affliction with the people of God rather than enjoy the pleasures of sin for a season. It goes on to say that by faith they kept the Passover and the sprinkling of blood. He goes on to say by faith they crossed the Red Sea. But did you ever notice when you read this passage that after they crossed the Red Sea not one thing that happened for the next 40 years made it in to the great hall of faith that happened as a result of faith?

I think the reason that nothing makes it into the great hall of faith is because the moment they crossed the Red Sea, they were at the foot of Mount Sinai where God gave the law. Once the law was given, faith shut down. God brought the children of Israel out of Egypt based on the Abrahamic covenant. All the Abrahamic covenant required was that you believe. God wanted to make an entire nation of priests. He wanted to have a personal relationship with every one of them where he would be to them a God and they would be to him a people. When God came down on Mount Sinai and the mountain was surrounded by smoke like the smoke of a great furnace, the mount burned with fire. The people then said to Moses, "We afraid of him. You go talk to him and whatever he says to you, we will do it. And if we do it, it will be our righteousness". They forfeited a personal relationship with God for a mediator system. Scripture tells us in Galatians that the law was added because of transgression. I submit to you that transgression was not just Adam's transgression. It was the transgression of the Abrahamic covenant. They failed to believe God.

When you forfeit a personal relationship with God, you must have rules. The less relationship you have the more rules you must have. Therefore, God gave the law. But that was not his best plan for them. Galatians tells us that the law was added "until" the seed should come to whom the promise was made. That seed was Christ. Christ was the end of the law for righteousness to everyone who believes. The new covenant is based on faith. Faith restores us to a relationship with God where we are led by the Spirit and not by rules. We walk with God in the cool of the day and live by every word that proceeds from his mouth.

In the new covenant the priesthood of the believer is restored. Personal relationship with God is once again offered. The apostle Peter would say, you are a chosen generation, a royal priesthood, a holy nation; a priesthood after the order of Melchisedec that serves bread and wine. If you study church history you will find that not more than 300 years after the apostles died, once again men began to set up a hierarchical system and deny believers access to God. They denied the priesthood of the believer for a hierarchical system of priest. When Martin Luther came on the scene, the priesthood of the believer was restored. We now have access by faith into this grace. One of the major tenets of Martin Luther's theses was the just will live by faith.

From the time they crossed the Red Sea and came to Sinai where God gave the law, not one thing was mentioned in Hebrews chapter 11 that happened by faith. Forty years of silence and faith kicked back in under the leadership of Joshua. It says by faith the walls of Jericho fell, after they were compassed about seven days.

Joshua said to God, give me the strategy to take Jericho. God said to him, you must get the children of Israel to go in the same direction at the same time and march around the city seven times with their mouths shut. My question is, why did they have to keep their mouth shut? The answer to that is simple. It is because the law was given so that every mouth would be stopped, and all the world would become guilty before God. The purpose was so that they would recognize they needed a Savior.

19 Now we know that what things soever the law saith, it saith to them who are under the law: **that every mouth may be stopped,** *and all the world may become guilty before God.* Rom. 3:19 KJV

God told Joshua to tell the people to keep silent until they heard a long, loud blast from a ram's horn and then they were instructed to shout. A ram's horn comes from a dead male lamb. The ram's horn was used as a trumpet in the Old Testament. The ram's horn represented the message of death of a male lamb. In other words, the moment you hear the message of the finished work of Jesus Christ, who is the true Lamb of God, you hear the message of his death, burial, and resurrection. It will create a shout that will cause the walls of religion that have kept you from your promise land to collapse and fall and you will enter your promise land. I believe this book is sounding a ram's horn in your ears and a generation is getting ready to shout.

I do not think it is an accident that the next thing that happens in Hebrews chapter 11 is by faith the harlot Rahab perished not with them that believed not. She received the spies with peace. The first thing I want you to notice is he did not put some glow-in-the-dark patriarch in this verse. If that would have been the case, you would have thought, then I am totally disqualified. I am not a saint. Instead, he added Rahab who ran the best little brothel in Jericho. Rahab ultimately ended up in the lineage of Christ. She was also a Gentile, indicating that faith gives access to both Jews and Gentiles. It qualifies the unqualified. All she did was hang a scarlet-colored cord in her window so that every bit of light that filtered into her house came through that scarlet-colored cord of redemption. The redemption that is in Christ is inclusive to both Jews and Gentiles and is accessed by faith. Both Jew and Gentile can walk through the door, which is Christ Jesus, into the sheepfold and find pasture.

- The Good Samaritan -

25 And, behold, a certain lawyer stood up, and tempted him, saying, Master, what shall I do to inherit eternal life? 26 He said unto him, What is written in the law? how readest thou? 27 And he answering said, Thou shalt love the Lord thy God with all thy heart, and with all thy soul, and with all thy strength, and with all thy mind; and thy neighbour as thyself. 28 And he said unto him, Thou hast answered right: this do, and thou shalt live. 29 But he, willing to justify himself, said unto Jesus, And who is my neighbour? 30 And Jesus answering said, A certain man went down from Jerusalem to Jericho, and fell among thieves, which stripped him of his raiment, and wounded him, and departed, leaving him half dead. 31 And by chance there came down a certain priest that way: and when he saw him, he passed by on the other side.

32 And likewise a Levite, when he was at the place, came and looked on him, and passed by on the other side. 33 But a certain Samaritan, as he journeyed, came where he was: and when he saw him, he had compassion on him, 34 And went to him, and bound up his wounds, pouring in oil and wine, and set him on his own beast, and brought him to an inn, and took care of him. 35 And on the morrow when he departed, he took out two pence, and gave them to the host, and said unto him, Take care of him; and whatsoever thou spendest more, when I come again, I will repay thee. 36 Which now of these three, thinkest thou, was neighbour unto him that fell among the thieves? 37 And he said, He that shewed mercy on him. Then said Jesus unto him, Go, and do thou likewise. Luke 10:25-37 KJV

The first thing I want you to notice in this text is that there is a certain lawyer who stood up. This was not a lawyer like we have in our day. He was an expert in the law of Moses. He is not really looking for an answer.

He is trying to tempt Jesus.

This lawyer asked Jesus, what do I have to do to "inherit" eternal life? This question is kind of an oxymoron to me because, first, you do not do anything in order to inherit. Someone must die and leave you something. According to the book of Hebrews a will is not in effect until the death of the testator. The good news is we have a copy of our Father's will and testament called the Bible. It may do us good to read our copy of the will. If not, we will settle out of court and lose our inheritance. I have an attorney on retainer whose name is Jesus Christ the righteous. He has never lost a case. We have one of the richest inheritances afforded to humanity. The New Testament is his last will and testament. The good news is he wrapped himself in human flesh and came and died so we can get what is in the will. What is even more powerful is that he got back up from the dead to be the administrator of his own will to make sure you get what he said you can have. That inheritance is eternal life. Yes, that includes going to heaven. But it is also declaring the life of the coming age; the life lived in the new covenant in the present reality of the kingdom of God.

This lawyer asked Jesus a question about the law. Let me first say that Matthew, Mark, Luke, and John are in the New Testament, but they are still primarily in the old covenant because the new covenant was not inaugurated until the cross. This lawyer asked Jesus a legal question, while they were under the law. He asked him, what must I "do" to inherit eternal life? The response of Jesus was, what is written in the law? How do you read it? Jesus then proceeds to give him two of the commandments. But because this lawyer knew he did not meet the criteria under the law, he was willing to justify himself by saying, who is my neighbor? Jesus put the commandment to love the Lord your God with all your heart on the same level of importance with loving your neighbor. Jesus said in another place, if you bring your gift to the altar and remember there that you have ought against your brother, leave your gift at the altar and be reconciled first to your brother. He was showing them that worship is not only vertical. It is not just the rituals of a pious religious system. Worship is also horizontal. It is how you treat your neighbor. How can you say you love God whom you have not seen, and do not love your brother, whom you have seen?

These old covenant commandments are full of demands without any supply. In the new covenant Jesus says, *"A NEW commandment I give you that you love one another as I have loved you; by this shall all men know that you are my disciples, if you have love one to another"*. John 13:34 KJV The difference in the new commandment is Jesus says, "as I have loved you". In other words, our love for each other flows out of the love that we have received from him. I love him because he first loved me. In other words, God sheds abroad his love in our hearts by the Holy Ghost who gives us the supply and the ability to love the unlovable.

Another comparison between the old covenant and the new covenant is in Matthew 6 where Jesus said, forgive and it will be forgiven you. Remember, the book of Matthew is in the New Testament, but it is still in the old covenant. Jesus was born of a woman born under the law, so he was teaching what the law required. On the other hand, the apostle Paul, after the cross, tells us, *"Be ye kind one to another, tenderhearted, forgiving one another, even as God for Christ's sake hath forgiven you"*. Eph. 4:32 KJV In the old covenant you had to forgive in order to be forgiven. In the new covenant you forgive because you have already been forgiven. One is full of demand and the other is full of supply. When we realize how much we have been forgiven it should be easy for us to forgive others.

- He Fell Among Thieves -

In the above story of the Samaritan Jesus tells of a man who fell among thieves. I submit to you that the thieves he was talking about was the religious system that was offering some other way. They could give you all kind of rules that were full of demand, but they have no supply. Many today have been left bleeding and dying by the Jericho road by well-meaning religious people who could point out your problem; but offer nothing to remedy your condition. God is far more interested in healing your brokenness than he is in judging you for your sin.

This man was left stripped, wounded, bleeding and dying and when a Levite passed by. He crossed the street and went to the other side. Likewise, a priest came by and did the same. Have you ever been in a place where you were wounded, dying and half naked because of religion, and all your religious friends seemed to avoid you?

The Samaritan, on the other hand, takes him to an inn and says to the innkeeper, whatever it costs to make him better, I am willing to pay the price. Do you know that whatever it costs to make you whole again, Jesus is willing to pay the price? As a matter of fact, he has already paid the price for your restoration. I believe that this inn is a picture of the local church that is embracing the gospel of grace in this hour. God is raising up places where instead of pointing out your problems, they will pour in oil and wine.

Oil and wine are symbols of the anointing of the Holy Spirit. Oil and wine flow from Zion. Zion is a picture of the new covenant. Remember, Hebrews chapter 12 says you have come to Mount Zion.

The Samaritan in this story is Jesus. Remember, the Samaritans were hated by the Jews. As a matter of fact, they accuse Jesus of being a Samaritan in John 8:48. What he is simply pointing out to this lawyer is that *he* was the neighbor. He was the one they were supposed to love. If they would fall in love with him, it would heal the wounds and stop the bleeding that had been inflicted by the thief of religion. They could inherit eternal life. They too could love the unlovable. The door is wide open my friend. He is the straight gate and the narrow way that leads to life. His name is Jesus. If you enter through that door, you will find life and that more abundant. It will lead you to the good Shepherd.

CHAPTER 6
I AM THE GOOD SHEPHERD

11 I am the good shepherd: the good shepherd giveth his life for the sheep. 12 But he that is an hireling, and not the shepherd, whose own the sheep are not, seeth the wolf coming, and leaveth the sheep, and fleeth: and the wolf catcheth them, and scattereth the sheep. 13 The hireling fleeth, because he is an hireling, and careth not for the sheep. 14 I am the good shepherd, and know my sheep, and am known of mine. 15 As the Father knoweth me, even so know I the Father: and I lay down my life for the sheep. 16 And other sheep I have, which are not of this fold: them also I must bring, and they shall hear my voice; and there shall be one fold, and one shepherd. 17 Therefore doth my Father love me, because I lay down my life, that I might take it again. 18 No man taketh it from me, but I lay it down of myself. I have power to lay it down, and I have power to take it again. This commandment have I received of my Father. John 10:11-18 KJV

Remember, each time the gospel of John says, "I Am", it is always in contrast to something from the old covenant. In other words, you thought Moses was the light. He was not the light because it was Moses who accused you before the Father. Jesus said, do not think I will accuse you to the Father. There is one that accuses you, even Moses. Immediately after Jesus says to the woman caught in adultery, neither do I condemn you, go and sin no more, he says, "I am the light of the world". Moses was not the light. Jesus was the true light that lights every man that comes into the world.

You thought the natural temple was the temple of God, but that is not the temple. Jesus is the true temple of God. You thought natural birth was enough, Nicodemus, but that is not enough. You must be born again. You must have a supernatural birth. You thought the manna that fell in the wilderness was the bread from heaven, but that is not the true bread. Jesus said, I am the true bread.

In the above Scripture Jesus is stating the truth that he is the good Shepherd. Let us look at a few of the Scriptures and see who they thought were the true shepherds of Israel.

*1 Woe be unto the pastors that destroy and scatter the sheep of my pasture! saith the Lord. 2 Therefore thus saith the Lord God of Israel against the pastors that feed my people; Ye have scattered my flock, and driven them away, and have not visited them: behold, I will visit upon you the evil of your doings, saith the Lord. 3 And I will gather the remnant of my flock out of all countries whither I have driven them, and will bring them again to their folds; and they shall be fruitful and increase. 4 And I will set up shepherds over them which shall feed them: and they shall fear no more, nor be dismayed, neither shall they be lacking, saith the Lord. 5 Behold, the days come, saith the Lord, that I will raise unto **David a righteous Branch**, and a King shall reign and prosper, and shall execute judgment and justice in the earth. 6 In his days Judah shall be saved, and Israel shall dwell safely: and this is his name whereby he shall be called, THE Lord OUR RIGHTEOUSNESS. 7 Therefore, behold, the days come, saith the Lord, that they shall no more say, The Lord liveth, which brought up the children of Israel out of the land of Egypt; 8 But, The Lord liveth, which brought up and which led the seed of the house of Israel out of the north country, and from all countries whither I had driven them; and they shall dwell in their own land.* Jer. 23:1-8 KJV

The first thing I want you to see in this Scripture is that false shepherds scatter and destroy the flock. True shepherds gather and feed the flock. True shepherds will lead you into green pastures to restore your soul. They will bring you into a place of fruitfulness and increase. True shepherds remove fear, dismay, and lack. True shepherds bring salvation, safety, and execute judgment and justice in the earth. The true Shepherd in the above verse is the Lord our righteousness. It is none other than the Lord Jesus Christ

*25 Whom God hath set forth to be a propitiation through faith in his blood, **to declare his righteousness** for the remission of sins that are past, through the forbearance of God; 26 **To declare, I say, at this time his***

righteousness: that he might be just, and the justifier of him which believeth in Jesus. Rom. 3:25-26 KJV

*30 But of him are ye in Christ Jesus, who of God is **made unto us wisdom, and righteousness, and sanctification, and redemption**:* 1 Cor. 1:30 KJV

Jesus completely matches the criteria for a true Shepherd in the above Scriptures. He also completely fulfills the promise of judgment and justice in these Old Testament texts. He was wounded for our transgression. He was bruised for our iniquities. The chastisement for our peace was laid upon him and by his stripes we are healed. See Isaiah 53. He is truly the righteous branch of David in these verses. He is just in justifying the ungodly through faith.

*4 Now to him that worketh is the reward not reckoned of grace, but of debt. 5 But to him that worketh not, but believeth on him that justifieth the ungodly, his faith is counted for righteousness. 6 **Even as David also describeth the blessedness of the man, unto whom God imputeth righteousness without works***, Rom. 4:4-6 KJV

The religious leaders of Jesus' day were truly the evil shepherds. The rulers of the synagogue and the scribes and Pharisees were the blind leaders of the blind. Yes, they thought the teachers of the law were the shepherds, but they were not the *true* Shepherd of the sheep. Jesus said, "I Am the good Shepherd". Compare these two Scriptures below.

*6 Also the sons of the stranger, that join themselves to the Lord, to serve him, and to love the name of the Lord, to be his servants, every one **that keepeth the sabbath** from polluting it, and taketh hold of my covenant; 7 Even them will I bring to my holy mountain, and make them joyful in my house of prayer: their burnt offerings and their sacrifices shall be accepted upon mine altar; for **mine house shall be called an house of prayer for all people**. 8 The Lord God which gathereth the outcasts of Israel saith, **Yet will I gather others to him, beside those that are gathered unto him**. 9 All ye beasts of the field, come to devour, yea, all ye beasts in the forest. 10 **His watchmen are blind: they are all ignorant, they are all dumb dogs,*** *they cannot bark; sleeping, lying down, loving to slumber. 11 Yea, they are greedy dogs which can never have enough, **and they are shepherds that cannot understand: they all look to their own way, every one for his gain,** from his quarter.* Isa. 56:6-11 KJV

*14 Let them alone: **they be blind leaders of the blind.** And if the blind lead the blind, both shall fall into the ditch.* Matt. 15:14 KJV

- Beware of Dogs -

First, let me point out some comparisons. In Matthew he is talking about the scribes and Pharisees. He calls them the blind leaders of the blind. In the Isaiah passage his watchmen are blind. They are all ignorant and dumb dogs. Perhaps these dogs are the people that the apostle Paul warned about in his letter to the Philippians. When he said, "beware of dogs, beware of the concision". He was not talking about Rover laying on your porch. He calls these religious leaders, dumb dogs.

Perhaps this is the same group that is outside the city in Revelation chapter 22. Outside the city were dogs and whoremongers and whoever loves the lie. Perhaps he is talking about the dog's nation of Israel and their false shepherds. They are outside the city. In the book of Revelation written earlier in this book; the city of God is not a place. It is a people. It is the bride, the Lamb's wife. It is the fulfillment of the Hebrews chapter 12 passage that said, for you have come to Mount Zion and you have already come to the city of the living God.

When writing to the church at Philadelphia in the book of Revelation chapter 3, he says to them, *"Him that overcomes will I make a pillar in the temple of my God, and he shall go no more out: and I will write upon him the name of my God, and the name of the city of my God, which is new Jerusalem, which cometh down out of heaven from my God: and I will write upon him my new name."* Rev.3:12 KJV In this verse he is not talking about a physical building or a physical city. He is talking about a spiritual temple and a spiritual city. He clearly tells them; I will write upon you the name of the city of my God. Then he tells them that the name of that city is New Jerusalem.

He also tells them in Matthew chapter 7 not to give that which is holy to dogs and do not cast your pearls before swine. He is not talking about animals in this verse. He is talking about people who have no value. The pearl of great price speaks of Christ's gift of salvation. As a matter of fact, the gates of the city in the book of Revelation are made of pearl. Consider the possibility that the pearly gates are not just a description of heaven somewhere off in the distant future. Consider the possibility that they speak of the salvation that came through his suffering when he became the door and the gate by which you enter the city of God.

The next thing I want to point out in the above Isaiah passage was the inclusion of the stranger. The inclusion of the stranger speaks of God including the Gentiles. It was the mystery that was hid from ages; but was now being make known. Those who would keep Sabbath would be made joyful. They would also be brought to the holy mountain. In that day, his house would be called a house of prayer. Is that not what Jesus said right after he cleansed the temple, my house shall be called house of prayer, but you have made it a den of thieves. It was in that context that Jesus declared, destroy this temple and in three days I will raise it back again. The temple we are being brought to in this hour is being made a part of the body of Christ, a spiritual house built upon the foundation of the apostles and prophets, Jesus Christ himself being the chief cornerstone. The holy mountain we have been brought to is Mount Zion, the city of the living God. Remember, Zion and the city of God represent the new covenant in contrast to Mount Sinai in Hebrews chapter 12.

- The Sabbath Is a Person -

The next thing I want you to see in the above Isaiah text is the blessing of keeping Sabbath. Now, before you think I am going to take you back to the law of Moses and argue over which day of the week we should keep, I want you to realize that in the new covenant the Sabbath is not a day of the week. It is a person. His name is Jesus. The Sabbath speaks of entering into his rest. We enter into his Sabbath rest. Then we realize that the work has been finished. A Revelation of the finished work of Jesus Christ will truly bring you into rest. Remember in Genesis when God created the heavens and the earth. He said thus the heavens and the earth were finished and all the host of them. On the seventh day God ended his work which he made. He rested on the seventh day from all his work. God himself rests in the knowledge that through Jesus Christ the work has been finished. He invites us into this Sabbath rest, because the work has been finished.

When God brought the children of Israel out of Egypt, he instituted Sabbath rest. He did not intend for it to become legalistic. He did that to show the children of Israel that he was not like the Egyptian slave masters. He did not want to drive them to work, day and night. He wanted them to have a day of rest. Look at the words of Jesus in this verse.

27 And he said unto them, The sabbath was made for man, and not man for the sabbath: 28 Therefore the Son of man is Lord also of the sabbath. Mark 2:27-28 KJV

Something greater than the Sabbath was on the scene. Jesus was Lord even of the Sabbath. As you read through the gospel you will quickly discover that Jesus did more miracles on the Sabbath day than any other day. For an in-depth study of this see my book titled *Unforced Rhythms of Grace*. All these miracles point to something that Jesus does from the posture of rest. A crooked woman is made straight. A withered hand is restored. A man born blind is healed. A man with dropsy is healed. A man by the pool of Bethesda is healed. The woman bowed to the earth is a picture of the church that is focused on the realm of the earth, all that is in the realm of the dust. Jesus says to this woman, you are loosed from this infirmity; stand upright. The withered hand speaks of the five-fold ministry with its five fingers of apostles, prophets, evangelists, pastors, and teachers. If they are not flowing from the posture of rest, they are withered. I won't go into all of these in this book because I have written extensively about them in other volumes. Suffice to say one greater than the Sabbath was on the scene. His name is Jesus and last, but not least, this verse in Colossians makes it clear that Jesus was the fulfillment and the substance of the Sabbath day.

*16 So let no one judge you in food or in drink, or regarding a festival or a new moon or sabbaths, 17 which are a shadow of things to come, **but the substance is of Christ***. Col. 2:16-17 NKJV

Yes, there is truly a blessing to honoring the Sabbath day. However, my view of honoring the Sabbath day is to honor what Jesus did in his finished work and let everything I do, flow from rest. Violating the Sabbath day would be thinking your works and labor could earn God's favor. Remember, in Genesis God finished the work. Right in the middle of the finished work he planted a garden and told the man all you must do is guard and keep what I have already done. Live out of relationship with me. Walk with me in the cool of the day and you will find rest for your soul.

- The Lord Is My Shepherd -

David probably capitalized on the idea of the true Shepherd more than anyone else in the Scriptures probably because he himself was a Shepherd King. He knew what it meant to care for sheep. Now the greater son of David, the Lord Jesus Christ, is the Shepherd of the sheep. His sheep hear his voice, and another they will not follow. Let us do a verse by verse study of Psalm chapter 23.

23 The Lord is my shepherd; I shall not want. Ps. 23:1 KJV

If the Lord is your Shepherd, you will lack for nothing. *I shall not want* does not mean you do not have a desire. It simply means he supplies all your needs according to his riches in glory. He does more than just supply your need. The psalmist declares in Psalm chapter 37 if you delight yourself in the Lord, he will give you the desire of your heart. If you truly delight in him, your desires will become his desires. You will live in abundance. That is what the abundant life is about. It is the days of heaven on earth. It is living in a land that flows with milk and honey. Look at what God said to Noah when he came forth out of the Ark into a new world.

7 You're here to bear fruit, reproduce, lavish life on the Earth, live bountifully!" Gen. 9:7 MSG

This sounds to me like God's original intention when he placed man in the garden. This sounds like his intention when he brought the children of Israel out of Egypt. He said to them I want to bring you into a land that flows with milk and honey. I want to give you the days of heaven on earth. Then Jesus came preaching the Kingdom and declared once again, I want you to have abundant life. It all began in a garden in Genesis, but because of the fall the garden, became a wilderness. In the New Testament Jesus came out of the wilderness and began his mission of new creation. Everything he did in his redemptive work he did in a garden. He prayed in a garden. He prayed until he sweat blood drops. He had to sweat and he had to bleed, because if he did and one drop of blood from the divine brow ever touched a cursed earth, it will put the curse in reverse that says, you must earn your bread by the sweat of your brow. You have been redeemed from having to work in order to gain God's favor. Adam had access to a tree of life, but he chose a tree of death. Jesus chose a tree of death and turned it into a tree of life. Jesus was buried in a garden because God was planting the new seed of the new creation. In the tomb of Joseph of Arimathea, three days later that graveyard became a garden. When Mary walked up to Jesus, she supposed him to be the gardener. He in fact *was* the gardener. God had put them back in a finished work in the garden. Genesis began in a garden and in Revelation chapters 21-22 it ends with a city in a garden. Two things are noticeably missing from the garden in Revelation. It has no serpent and no tree of the knowledge of good and evil. I am glad the Lord is my Shepherd and that my God shall supply all my needs according to his riches in glory by Christ Jesus.

- Green Pastures -

2 He maketh me to lie down in green pastures: he leadeth me beside the still waters. Ps. 23:2 KJV

I must mention here that the Lord is your Shepherd and he always takes you to a place of rest where you can lie down in green pastures. It is the place he restores your soul.

In Revelation chapter 4 of the heavenly vision of the throne, John the revelator declares, I saw a rainbow around about the throne in sight like unto an emerald. The rainbow is a symbol of the covenant. Remember the covenant God made with Noah. This rainbow was the token of the covenant. It is the same rainbow that is round about the throne in Revelation 4:3. The throne represents the Kingdom and the rainbow represents the covenant through which the Kingdom operates, namely, the new covenant. It is the color of an emerald and an emerald is green. Green symbolizes the new covenant.

Remember in Genesis it says the end of all flesh is come before me, because the earth is full of violence. God was about to remove an old world dominated by sin and the curse and bring Noah into a new world. Hebrews chapter 11 says by faith Noah built an Ark to the saving of his house. I say to every leader in this hour we must build something redemptive. God's method of salvation was an Ark.

That Ark is an old testament type and shadow of Christ. He is our Ark of safety and he is our vehicle out of an old world dominated by sin. God instructed Noah to make an Ark out of shittim wood. If you are going to build something redemptive you are going to have to involve a tree. That Ark of safety, and that tree in the New Testament is found on Golgotha's Hill. It is an old rugged cross.

It is not an accident that the dimensions of the Ark were 30 cubits, by 50 cubits, by 300 cubits. Even the numerology in this text is symbolic. The Bible number 30 means the blood of Christ, the number 50 means Pentecost and the number 300 means divine completeness. It is through the blood of Jesus and the power of the Holy Ghost that he brings us to divine completeness.

This Ark had three stories much like the tabernacle of Moses had three courts. This Ark had one window above so that if you were going to look out, you must look up. It had one door, and that door was Jesus. God told

99

Noah to pitch it within and without with pitch. Interesting enough the Hebrew word for pitch is a word we translate atonement other places in the Scripture, because what seals us in and seals the world out is the precious atoning blood of Jesus. What I want you to see is that those in the Ark did not escape the judgment of God. Everyone on the Ark was inside of the thing the judgment fell upon, just like we were in Christ. When he took on himself all our judgment, we identified with his death in water baptism. The apostle Peter identifies the Ark of Noah with water baptism.

*20 Which sometime were disobedient, when once the longsuffering of God waited in the **days of Noah, while the ark was a preparing, wherein few, that is, eight souls were saved by water.***

*21 **The like figure whereunto even baptism doth also now save us** (not the putting away of the filth of the flesh, but the answer of a good conscience toward God,) by the resurrection of Jesus Christ:* 1 Peter 3:20-21 KJV

Two birds flew out of the Ark of Noah searching for the new world. One of them flew all the way through the Scriptures and landed in the book of Revelation where Babylon became the hold of every foul spirit and the cage of every unclean and hateful bird. But the dove only had to fly to the book of Matthew where it found Jesus coming up out of the waters of baptism. When the dove landed on Jesus it signified to John the Baptist, right here is the new world, right here is where the curse has been reversed. Interesting enough it was when Jesus came up out of the waters of baptism. In Genesis, the Ark comes to rest on a mountain called Ararat. The word Ararat means the curse has been reversed.

In Matthew chapter 24 Jesus said to that first-century audience, as it was in the days of Noah so shall it be in the days of the coming of the Son of Man. He was talking about his coming in judgment upon the apostate nation of Israel in A.D. 70. He was warning first-century Jews to get on board this redemptive ark because an old world and an old creation was about to be removed once again. A new creation was about to be birthed.

The curse was about to be reversed for all those who could get on board this Ark of safety. Many in the first century did not heed his voice. They missed the boat. Matthew 24:38-39 says *"For as in the days that were before the flood they were eating and drinking, marrying and giving in marriage, until the day Noah entered the Ark and knew not until the flood came and took them all away; so shall also the coming of the Son of Man be."* The door of the Ark was about to be closed to the nation of Israel and the first century was about to be swept away by the flood of the Roman soldiers that would come and take them all away. Please notice in Matthew chapter 24 it is not the righteous that are taken away. It is the wicked that are removed, just like it was in the days of Noah.

But Noah found "grace" in the eyes of the Lord. God removed that old system of the curse and replaced it with grace and favor. I do not know about you, but I do not want to miss this boat. That ship has sailed, and we are on our way to the other side where there is no curse. In the story of Noah God cleanses the earth with a flood. In the new covenant, he cleanses us with his blood. The rainbow symbolizes God's everlasting covenant. It is the token of the covenant.

*13 I do set my bow in the cloud, and it shall be **for a token of a covenant** between me and the earth. 14 And it shall come to pass, when I bring a cloud over the earth, that the bow shall be seen in the cloud: 15 **And I will remember my covenant**, which is between me and you and every living creature of all flesh; and the waters shall no more become a flood to destroy all flesh. 16 And the bow shall be in the cloud; and I will look upon it, that I may remember the everlasting covenant between God and every living creature of all flesh that is upon the earth. 17 And God said unto Noah, This is the token of the covenant, which I have established between me and all flesh that is upon the earth.* Gen. 9:13-17 KJV

Isaiah chapter 53 is the story of the redemptive work of Christ. He was wounded for our transgressions; he was bruised for our iniquities. Chastisement from peace was upon him. Right behind that story God said, this is as the waters of Noah to me. My question is, what was like the waters of Noah? The answer is Jesus in his redemptive work has redeemed us from the curse of the law. The curse has been reversed.

*7 For a small moment have I forsaken thee; but with great mercies will I gather thee. 8 In a little wrath I hid my face from thee for a moment; but with everlasting kindness will I have mercy on thee, saith the Lord thy Redeemer. 9 **For this is as the waters of Noah unto me**: for as I have sworn that the waters of Noah should no more go over the earth; so have I sworn that I would not be wroth with thee, nor rebuke thee. 10 For the mountains shall depart, and the hills be removed; but my kindness shall not depart from thee, neither shall the covenant of my peace be removed, saith the Lord that hath mercy on thee. Isa. 54:7-10 KJV*

Isaiah 54:1 starts out by saying, *"Sing, o barren, and you that did not bare"*. The Apostle Paul quotes this verse in Galatians 4:27 in the context of talking about removing the old Jerusalem and the old covenant and replacing it with the new covenant messianic Kingdom of Christ.

*24 Now all this is an allegory; these [two women] represent two covenants. One covenant originated from Mount Sinai [where the Law was given] and bears [children destined] for slavery; this is Hagar. 25 Now Hagar is (stands for) Mount Sinai in Arabia and she corresponds to and belongs in the same category **with the present Jerusalem**, for she is in bondage together with her children. 26 **But the Jerusalem above (the Messianic kingdom of Christ) is free, and she is our mother.**_27 For it is written in the Scriptures, **Rejoice, O barren woman**, who has not given birth to children; break forth into a joyful shout, you who are not feeling birth pangs, for the desolate woman has many more children than she who has a husband. [Isa 54:1.] 28 But we, brethren, are children [not by physical descent, as was Ishmael, but] like Isaac, born in virtue of promise. 29 Yet [just] as at that time the child [of ordinary birth] born according to the flesh despised and persecuted him [who was born remarkably] according to [the promise and the working of] the [Holy] Spirit, so it is now also. [Gen 21:9.] 30 **But what does the Scripture say? Cast out and send away the slave woman and her son, for never shall the son of the slave woman be heir and share the inheritance with the son of the free woman.** [Gen 21:10.] 31 So, brethren, **we [who are born again]** are not* *children of a slave woman [the natural], but of the free [the supernatural].* Gal. 4:24-31 AMP

Yes, the Lord is my Shepherd. He makes me lie down in green pastures. This chapter should make it clear to you exactly what it means to lie down in green pastures. It means to come into a full revelation of the finished work of Jesus Christ and let him who is the good Shepherd feed you on new covenant truth. You will truly find rest for your soul.

In Song of Solomon the bride declares, "behold our bed is green". The bed symbolizes the place of rest and the place of reproduction.

In Psalm 92:10 the psalmist declares, "I shall be anointed with fresh oil". The Hebrew word for fresh in this text literally means *green*. The psalmist is saying I will be anointed with green oil. What that says to me is that there is a fresh anointing that was coming, and that anointing was a new covenant anointing. Oh, that God would anoint his ministers today with the green anointing of new covenant truth. Only then as under-shepherds will we be able to bring God's people into rest in green pastures. Then we will be able to bring them into the very throne room of God with its green rainbow. Only then will his Bride be able to find rest and declare our bed is green. Surely the Lord is my Shepherd. He makes me lie down in green pastures.

- He Restores My Soul -

3 He *restoreth my soul: he leadeth me in the paths of righteousness for his name's sake.* Ps. 23:3 KJV

An entire volume should be written on this subject, but I will try to be brief here. God's plan of redemption includes redeeming us spirit, soul, and body. See I Thessalonians 5:23. The word soul in the Greek language is a word that we translate as *psyche*. It has to do with our mind, will and emotions. It is translated in the King James Bible in a couple of different ways. It is translated as heart, mind, soul; but it is also translated *life*. The restoration of my soul is to return me back to my right mind; to think properly, to think like God thinks. Let this mind be in you which was also in Christ Jesus. The right mind is the mind of Christ. When you have the mind of Christ, he will give you back your life. The restoration of your soul is the restoration of your life. Right thinking will produce a quality of life. I must say that since I have had a revelation of the new covenant and the grace of God, my life has been so much better than I could have ever imagined. I truly am enjoying the journey.

The entire chapter of Hebrews 4 talks about rest. It is in the context of rest in the finished work of Jesus Christ, that he says:

*12 For the word of God is quick, and powerful, and sharper than any twoedged sword, piercing even to the dividing asunder **of soul and spirit**, and of the joints and marrow, and is a discerner of the **thoughts and intents of the heart**. 13 Neither is there any creature that is not manifest in his sight: but all things are naked and opened unto the eyes of him with whom we have to do. 14 Seeing then that we have a great high priest, that is passed into the heavens, Jesus the Son of God, let us hold fast our profession. 15 For we have not an high priest which cannot be touched with the feeling of our infirmities; but was in all points tempted like as we are, yet without sin. 16 Let us therefore come boldly unto the throne of grace, that we may obtain mercy, and find grace to help in time of need.* Heb. 4:12-16 KJV

Rest reveals what is in your heart. When I first started preaching grace and the new covenant, I started seeing people act in ways that was not becoming to Saints. I became concerned and thought, am I preaching something that makes people want to sin? I was tempted to go back and preach a little bit of law just to get people to behave. You see, law will change your behavior, but grace will change your heart. It will save your soul.

The Lord said to me, the word is doing exactly what it is supposed to do . The word that flows from rest will reveal what is in your heart. It is not so you can act on it and destroy your life or someone else's. It is revealed so that he can lead you in the path of righteousness for his name sake. You see, you do not become righteous by works. But there is works of righteousness. It is the works that flow from the revelation that I am already righteous because of the work of Calvary.

The word that flows from rest reveals your heart, not so you can act on it, but so that you can come boldly to a throne of grace. It is not a throne of judgment, but a throne of grace. It is there that you will obtain mercy and find grace to help in time of need. You will find a faithful high priest who can be touched with the feeling of your infirmities, because he was tempted in all points just like we were yet without sin. Grace does not cause sin. It is the antidote for it. Where sin abounds that is where grace will super-abound. The book of Titus declares the grace of God has appeared to all men, teaching us to deny ungodliness. Grace is a teacher. When he makes you lie down in green pastures, it will restore your soul and truly lead you in the path of righteousness. It is for his name sake. Remember, the purpose of the book of John is that in believing, you might have life through his name.

- The Valley of the Shadow of Death -

4 Yea, though I walk through the valley of the shadow of death, I will fear no evil: for thou art with me; thy rod and thy staff they comfort me. Ps. 23:4 KJV

The key word in this verse is *through*, yea, although I walk *through* the Valley of the shadow of death. I believe the reason David called it the shadow was because the old testament was the shadow and the New Testament is the substance. The shadow of the death that he was talking about was the death of Christ. He was living in the shadow. We live in the reality of his death and finished work. It is because of that I fear no evil. He is with me and in the New Testament he will never leave me, nor forsake me. His rod and his staff speak of the shepherd's hook that reaches out. When I stray away from the flock, he draws me back in. I am comforted by his correction.

105

- A Table in the Presence of My Enemies -

5 Thou preparest a table before me in the presence of mine enemies: thou anointest my head with oil; my cup runneth over. Ps. 23:5 KJV

The table he prepares in the presence of my enemies is the communion table. It is the covenant meal. The Holy Spirit said to me, "you ate your way into this problem, you can eat your way out". He said it all started with an eating disorder in Eden's misty garden when I said, do not eat from the tree the knowledge of good and evil. The tree of the knowledge of good and evil represents the law. For by the law is the knowledge of sin. There is a completely different tree from which we must feed.

When the children of Israel were about to leave Egypt, Moses said to God, give me the strategy for what it takes to leave Egypt. God told him to take a lamb inside the house and eat it in the night roasted with fire. He told him to eat the whole lamb. I am convinced that if we will feed people on a steady diet of Lamb, about midnight something will hit them that says I cannot live in this bondage any longer. No matter what kind of bondage you are in, there is something on the table that can bring you freedom and deliverance. What you feed on produces either life or death. Much of what is served over American pulpits in this hour is the sweet treats of spiritual Twinkies and potato chips. For a while it will make people bounce off the walls. But it has no nutritional value and will not bring deliverance in their lives. A steady diet of the finished work of Jesus Christ will lead you through any valley you encounter. There is always something on the table that you can feed on that will bring deliverance.

When we consider the valley of the shadow of the death, remember the night before Jesus was crucified. They were in an upper room. It was his last night on planet earth. He knew it was his last night with his disciples. What would you do if it were your last night on the planet and you knew it? Jesus said to his disciples, with great desire have I desired to keep this Passover with you. In other words, "let's eat.". Jesus knew that this would be the last time they would ever have to kill a physical lamb. From the Passover, Jesus in his death, burial and resurrection was the final Lamb of

God. Every time we come to the table, we must serve bread and wine of the new covenant. We must feed on his finished work and it will anoint our head with oil until our cup runs over. Perhaps the oil that he anoints our head with is the green oil that I mentioned earlier in this chapter: the new anointing of the new covenant. Oh, God, anoint our heads with oil. Truly the Lord is the good Shepherd. The sheep hear his voice, and another they will not follow. When we follow him, surely goodness and mercy will follow all the days of our life and we will dwell in the house of the Lord forever.

CHAPTER 7
I AM THE RESURRECTION AND THE LIFE

The next time Jesus makes the statement "I Am" is in the context of the story of Lazarus.

*23 Jesus saith unto her, Thy brother shall rise again. 24 Martha saith unto him, I know that he shall rise again in the resurrection at the last day. 25 Jesus said unto her, **I am the resurrection, and the life**: he that believeth in me, though he were dead, yet shall he live: 26 And whosoever liveth and believeth in me shall never die. Believest thou this?* John 11:23-26 KJV

The story begins with Lazarus being sick. He was the brother of Mary, who anointed the feet of Jesus and wiped his feet with her hair. Mary sent word to Jesus telling him, he whom you love is sick. Jesus declared, "This sickness is not unto death, but for the glory of God, that the son of God might be glorified."

When Jesus heard that Lazarus was sick, he stayed two days in the same place where he was. Then he said to his disciples, let us go into Judea again. But the disciples were concerned because as of late the Jews had sought to stone him. Jesus then said to the disciples, "Our friend Lazarus sleeps; but I go, that I may awaken him out of sleep." The disciples thought Jesus was talking about Lazarus resting Then Jesus spoke plainly to them, "Lazarus is dead." He said to them, "I am glad for your sakes, that I was not there to the intent that you may believe. Nevertheless, let us go to him."

When Jesus got to Bethany, he discovered that Lazarus had been in the grave for four days. Martha said to Jesus, Lord, if you had only been here my brother would not have died. Jesus replied to her, your brother will rise again.

The first thing I want you to notice is that Lazarus was in the grave four days. Lazarus to me is a picture of humanity that had been dead four days.

Think of it in terms of thousand-year days. Peter said, a day with the Lord is 1000 years and 1000 years is as a day. When Jesus came on the scene humanity had been dead four thousand years or, if you will, four days. Jesus came to awaken from the sleep of death all that would believe. For by one man death came upon all men.

12 Wherefore, as by one man sin entered into the world, and death by sin; and so death passed upon all men, for that all have sinned: 13 (For until the law sin was in the world: but sin is not imputed when there is no law. 14 Nevertheless death reigned from Adam to Moses, even over them that had not sinned after the similitude of Adam's transgression, who is the figure of him that was to come. 15 But not as the offence, so also is the free gift. For if through the offence of one many be dead, much more the grace of God, and the gift by grace, which is by one man, Jesus Christ, hath abounded unto many. Rom. 5:12-15 KJV

Yes, humanity had been dead four days. Then they said to him, by now he stinks. Truly the smell of the bondage of decay was everywhere. Dead rotten stinking flesh had permeated the human family. But Jesus is the only one I know of that can be four days late and still be on time. Jesus said to them, show me where you have laid him. This is one of the only places in the Scripture that is recorded that Jesus wept. The Jews thought he wept because of how much he loved Lazarus, but I believe he was weeping because of their unbelief.

- Take Away the Stone -

The stone in this story represents the law. The law was written on stone tablets. Remember in the above verse sin was not imputed where there was no law. The law is what gives sin strength. It is what gives death a sting. It is what we preach over pulpits every week.

56 The sting of death is sin; and the strength of sin is the law. 1 Cor. 15:56 KJV

Jesus came to roll the stone away. I believe it is the job of every valid five-fold new covenant ministry to roll the stone away. It is our job to remove the grave clothes of a religious system that has kept people bound for centuries. We must loose them and let them go. I am not suggesting we roll the stone of the law to release dead, stinking flesh. I am suggesting we roll the stone of the law away to release the power of the resurrected life. Once again, the comparison that I want to make in this chapter is they search the Scriptures. For in them they thought they had eternal life. They were looking in the old covenant texts for life, but it could not give them life. It gave sin power and death a sting. In other words, you thought the old covenant was the source of life, but that is not the source of resurrection of life. Jesus said, I am the resurrection and the life.

16 And not as it was by one that sinned, so is the gift: for the judgment was by one to condemnation, but the free gift is of many offences unto justification. 17 For if by one man's offence death reigned by one; much more **they which receive abundance of grace and of the gift of righteousness shall reign in life by one, Jesus Christ.** *18 Therefore as by the offence of one judgment came upon all men to condemnation; even so by the righteousness of one the free gift came upon all men unto justification of life. 19 For as by one man's disobedience many were made sinners, so by the obedience of one shall many be made righteous. 20 Moreover the law entered,* **that the offence might abound. But where sin abounded, grace did much more abound:** *21* **That as sin hath reigned unto death, even so might grace reign through righteousness unto eternal life by Jesus Christ our Lord.** Rom. 5:16-21 KJV

I truly hope as you read this book that it will help you to be able to roll the stone of the law away from your own life, then from the life of others.

6 Who also hath made us able ministers of the new testament; not of the letter, but of the spirit: **for the letter killeth, but the spirit giveth life.** *7 But if the* **ministration of death, written and engraven in stones,** *was glorious, so that the children of Israel could not stedfastly behold the face of Moses for the glory of his countenance; which glory was to be done away: 8 How shall not the ministration of the spirit be rather glorious?* 2 Cor. 3:6-8 KJV

Martha had the perception that resurrection was an event in the last day. But Jesus would reveal in this story that the resurrection is more than just a one-time event. It is a person. It is a person named Jesus. Jesus said to her, the hour is coming. Yes, there is a resurrection in the future; however, it is not just a future event. It is a present reality for believers.

*25 Jesus said unto her, **I am the resurrection, and the life**: he that believeth in me, though he were dead, yet shall he live: 26 And whosoever liveth and believeth in me shall never die. Believest thou this?* John 11:25-26 KJV

The question is do you believe this? Remember, John states the purpose of this book is that, believing, you would have life through his name. Not just life when you die, but right now. Sometimes I think we hesitate to roll the stone of the law away because we are afraid it will release the stench of dead, stinking flesh.

Because we refuse to roll the stone of the law away, we keep people captive to the very thing that produces death in their lives. The greatest need of humanity is life. Adam released the force of death; Jesus released the force of life. Remember in the garden of Eden God said, in the moment you eat from the tree of the knowledge of good and evil you will surely die. Death was the result of feeding from the wrong tree. The Scripture says, if there was a commandment which could have given life, then righteousness would have been by the law. When the man and his wife ate from the wrong tree, the Lord sent them forth from the Garden of Eden to till the ground. The result was earning your bread by the sweat of your brow. Jesus sweat great drops of blood in the Garden of Gethsemane to redeem us from ever having to earn God's favor again. He sweated so that I do not have to.

- Coats of Skin -

I do not believe that God sent them out of the garden to punish them. I think he sent them out of the garden to protect them. He did it so they would not eat of the tree of life and live forever in a fallen condition.

Perhaps the coats of skin he gave them was the skin we now have on our human bodies. God gave them coats of skin so that the shame of their nakedness would not appear. Perhaps he gave them an earthly body; one capable of death and decay. The apostle Paul uses the same terminology when he talks about receiving our house which is from heaven, that is our spiritual house, when he makes this statement:

*1 For we know that if **our earthly house of this tabernacle** were dissolved, we have a building of God, an house not made with hands, eternal in the heavens. 2 For in this we groan, earnestly desiring to be clothed upon with our house which is from heaven:*

*3 **If so be that being clothed we shall not be found naked.** 4 For we that are in this tabernacle do groan, being burdened: not for that we would be unclothed, but clothed upon, that mortality might be swallowed up of life.* 2 Cor. 5:1-4 KJV

Perhaps one of the things Adam lost in the fall was a spiritual body. One of the things that Jesus restores in the new creation is the spiritual body. The apostle Paul writes in 1 Corinthians chapter 15 that there is a celestial body and a terrestrial body. In the context of the resurrection of the dead he said, it is sown in dishonor and it is raised in glory. It is sown in weakness and it is raised in power. It is sown a natural body and is raised a spiritual body. There is a natural body and there is a spiritual body. It is written that the first Adam was made a living soul and the last Adam was made a quickening spirit. The first man was out of the earth and he was earthy. The second man is the Lord from heaven. We bore the image of the earthy and shall also bear the image of the heavenly.

Perhaps what Adam had before the fall was a celestial body. One thing I am certain of is that in the new covenant he brought life and immortality to light through the gospel. There has not been a believer that has truly died in 2000 years. That is what Jesus was saying to them at the tomb of Lazarus when he said, if you live and believe in me, you will never die. Death has been abolished. The covenant of death has been removed. If that is not what Jesus meant at the tomb of Lazarus, then no one has lived

112

and believed in him for 2000 years and counting.

- We Will Not All Sleep -

When the apostle Paul said in I Corinthians chapter 15, we shall not all sleep, but we will be changed, he was telling the church at Corinth that something had occurred after the resurrection of Jesus that was not possible under the old covenant. In the old covenant the moment you died the Scripture says, that they slept with their fathers. In other words, they were waiting on a resurrection. They were waiting on the covenant of death to be disannulled. They were waiting on someone with the keys of hell and of death to descend into the lower parts of the earth and lead captivity captive. These all died in faith, not receiving the promise. Prior to the resurrection of Jesus, no man had ascended into heaven, but he that came down from heaven, even the Son of Man which was in heaven. So, the way into heaven was not yet made.

Jesus, however, was the first fruits of them that slept. When he got up from the dead and came out of the grave many of the bodies of the Saints which slept arose and came out of the graves after his resurrection and went into the holy city and appeared to many. See Matthew 27:53-54. This was the first fruits of them that slept. When the resurrected Saints marched down the street of the holy city, it was the fulfillment of the wave of sheath of first fruit. It was declaring the resurrection has begun and is now underway. It is not an accident that the apostle Paul uses the harvest paradigm to describe the resurrection. He declares it is sown in weakness. It is raised in power since this was the fulfillment of the wave of sheath of first fruits. It would declare that a harvest would follow, a general resurrection. But there is an order to resurrection. Let us look at this verse.

*23 **But every man in his own order: Christ the firstfruits; afterward they that are Christ's at his coming**. 24 Then cometh the end, when he shall have delivered up the kingdom to God, even the Father; when he shall have put down all rule and all authority and power. 25 For he must reign, till he hath put all enemies under his feet.*

*26 **The last enemy that shall be destroyed is death.** 27 For he hath put all things under his feet. But when he saith, all things are put under him, it is manifest that he is excepted, which did put all things under him.* 1 Cor. 15:23-27 KJV

*10 But is now made manifest by the appearing of our Saviour Jesus Christ, **who hath abolished death, and hath brought life and immortality to light** through the gospel:* 2 Tim. 1:10 KJV

Please note the above verse did not say he is going to abolish death. It said he already has. Either it is finished, or it is not. Either we have resurrection life, or we do not. I believe we have it right now. Jesus did not say I am *going to be* the resurrection and the life someday. He said, "I am the resurrection and the life". We will either put on immortality and be swallowed up of life or we will put off this body and step into immortality. Either way, life and immortality are available right now to all who believe. Resurrection power entered me the moment I was born again. I passed from death unto life.

Remember, it took Adam 1000 years to die physically once death was released. Perhaps since Jesus released life and immortality, it will take 1000 years to learn how to live. I think it highly possible that a generation will walk into putting on their house which is from heaven, that is their new body on this side of the grave. Regardless of what the future holds, what I want us to see is that this life and immortality is available to us right now. It is inside of us. After all, we do not groan to be unclothed but to be clothed upon with our house which is from heaven. But if we put off the tabernacle of this house here, we have a building of God eternal in the heavens. It is a win-win situation. No matter what you believe, it is available right now.

The first thing I want you to notice is that the order to resurrection is as follows - Christ and the first fruits. The resurrection in Matthew chapter 27 would have to be the fulfillment of this Scripture. They were the first fruits of them that slept; afterward, they that are Christ's at his coming. I submit to you the possibility that it was his coming in judgment upon apostate

114

Israel in A.D. 70. If this is not true, then the second Scripture from the Timothy passage cannot be possible. It declares he has already abolished death and brought life and immortality to light through the gospel. Remember these Scriptures are written to a first-century audience. Now I know what you are thinking. You are thinking about this verse:

17 And their word will eat as doth a canker: of whom is Hymenaeus and Philetus; 18 Who concerning the truth have erred, **saying that the resurrection is past already**; *and overthrow the faith of some.* 2 Tim. 2:17-18 KJV

- Timing Is Everything -

If you are going to use this Scripture to try to prove me wrong, you must understand that this Scripture was written before A.D. 70. The first resurrection in Matthew chapter 27 would have occurred somewhere around A.D. 30. For the next 40 years, the writer of Hebrews declared that the first covenant was fading away. It would find its end in A.D. 70. The general resurrection would take place sometime after A.D. 70, at the last trumpet. But in Revelation chapter 11 the seventh trumpet, which is the last trumpet, sounds immediately after the temple is destroyed and the holy city trampled underfoot by the Gentiles for 42 months. The siege of Jerusalem by the Romans was 42 months. Immediately after the temple was destroyed in Revelation chapter 11, there is a resurrection.

18 And the nations were angry, and thy wrath is come, **and the time of the dead**, *that they should be judged, and that thou shouldest give reward unto thy servants the prophets, and to the saints, and them that fear thy name, small and great; and shouldest destroy them which destroy the earth.* Rev. 11:18 KJV

I must mention here that Jesus told his first-century followers that some of them would be alive at his coming. While my subject matter in this book is not the coming of the Lord, I must mention a few Scriptures that prove that there had to be some kind of the coming of the Lord in the first century. Either that or Jesus was a false prophet.

27 For the Son of man shall come in the glory of his Father with his angels; and then he shall reward every man according to his works. 28 Verily I say unto you, **There be some standing here, which shall not taste of death, till they see the Son of man coming in his kingdom.** Matt. 16:27-28 KJV

23 But when they persecute you in this city, flee ye into another: for verily I say unto you, **Ye shall not have gone over the cities of Israel, till the Son of man be come.** Matt. 10:23 KJV

34 Verily I say unto you, **This generation shall not pass, till all these things be fulfilled.** Matt. 24:34 KJV

*37 **FOR YET IN A VERY LITTLE WHILE, HE WHO IS COMING WILL COME, AND WILL NOT DELAY.** 38 BUT MY RIGHTEOUS ONE SHALL LIVE BY FAITH; AND IF HE SHRINKS BACK, MY SOUL HAS NO PLEASURE IN HIM.* Heb. 10:37-38 NASU

These are just a few Scriptures among many that should help us to consider at least the possibility that there was some type of fulfillment of his coming in the first century. I am not saying that it is not possible that Jesus is still coming in the future. I think he has appeared in different ways through history. In Revelation, he says, I am he which was, which is, and which is to come. He is the ever coming one. As a matter of fact, I think we use terminologies like his second coming when, in reality you find him coming many times in Scripture. The only place in the New Testament that talks about his second coming is in Hebrews chapter 9 and that verse was not talking about him coming in the clouds. It was talking about him as high priest appearing once in the end of the age of the law to put away sin by the sacrifice of himself. That is not something he is going to do. It is something he has already done. It is him fully meeting the appointment of death and judgment for all men. The imagery is drawn from the Old Testament high priest when he would go into the Most Holy Place with blood. The whole congregation of Israel would wait outside the tabernacle with bated breath to see if he would come back out. If he did not return a second time, that meant God had not put away their sin. If. Jesus has not already appeared a second time, we are still in our sin.

The reason you never find the terminology of his first coming in the Scripture is because it was not as a baby in a manger. He appeared to Abraham as Melchisedec. He was the ram caught in the thicket. He was the fourth man in the fire with Daniel, etc. He came throughout the Scriptures in many wonderful ways, in varying forms.

After his resurrection, he appeared to the disciples in an upper room. He appeared to the disciples on the road to Emmaus. He appeared to Apostle Paul when he knocked him to the ground. He walked through walls and ate with them. Jesus demonstrated that a spiritual body could take on many forms and appear and disappear at will. He promises us that we will have a body just like his glorious body.

Sometimes his appearing is visible and literal. Sometimes his appearing is spiritual. Sometimes his presence is there, yet you do not see him. As a matter of fact, the word that is translated for *coming* in many scriptures in the New Testament is the Greek word Parousia and can mean *his presence*. My point, I think sometimes we are so enamored with a coming Jesus that we forget about the one that is already here. We would rather have a Jesus who lives in the temple in Israel than the one who lives in the temple of my body right now. If he lived in the Middle East, I would have to fly there to see him. But since he lives in me, I have access to him always. I can come boldly to his throne at any given moment. I have access to the one who says, I will never leave you or forsake you. He is the one who lives and resides inside us. We sing to him like he is not in the room. Whose presence do you think it is that you feel when you sit in a service? This word for coming also speaks specifically of his return to punish Jerusalem. See the definition below for the word *coming*. This word is translated in the King James Version as coming, and presence.

NT:3952
<START GREEK>parousi/a

<END GREEK> parousia (par-oo-see'-ah); from the present participle of NT:3918; a being near, i.e. advent (often, return; specifically, of Christ to punish Jerusalem, or finally the wicked); (by implication) physically,

aspect:

KJV - coming, presence.

When the apostle Paul said, behold, I show you a mystery, we will not all sleep, he used a lot of personal pronouns like he was included in that promise. He was not saying that some of them would not face physical death, because Paul himself was martyred. What he was saying is, even if we do face physical death, we will not all sleep. Some of them would remain alive until the coming of the Lord in judgment in A.D. 70. From then on something had changed for those who were alive and remain until the coming of the Lord. Once that resurrection had taken place, believers would no longer sleep. We will be changed in a moment in the twinkling of an eye, at the last trump. He was saying that from the general resurrection in A.D. 70 of all those old covenant Saints who had died, we no longer sleep with the fathers. We no longer wait for resurrection. The moment we take our last breath we are immediately in the presence of the Lord.

If you have been with someone who is passing away, often they will begin to communicate with someone who has gone on before. They will see their husband, mother, father or a loved one. They may possibly see Jesus. They are not falling asleep. They are passing from death into life. That is why I prefer to call it passing away instead of dying. In 1 Thessalonians chapter 4 the apostle Paul once again uses personal pronouns. The chapter before and the chapter after I Thessalonians chapter 4 is all relevant to the first-century church at Thessalonica. Paul was not writing to us. He was writing to a first-century church and was saying to them, I do not want you to be ignorant concerning them who have fallen asleep. He was saying this to give comfort to those who were losing their loved ones to martyrdom, etc.

13 But I do not want you to be ignorant, brethren, concerning those who *have fallen asleep, lest you sorrow as others who have no hope. 14 For if we believe that Jesus died and rose again, even so God will bring with Him those who sleep in Jesus. 15 For this we say to you by the word of the Lord, that we who are alive and remain until the coming of the Lord will by no means precede those who are asleep. 16 For the Lord Himself will descend from heaven with a shout, with the voice of an archangel, and with the trumpet of God. And the dead in Christ will rise first. 17 Then we who **are alive and remain** shall be caught up together with them in the **clouds to meet o the Lord in the air**. And thus we shall always be with the Lord. 18 Therefore comfort one another with these words.* 1 Thess. 4:13-18 NKJV

This Scripture is about resurrection. Paul is describing what would happen to those who were falling asleep in this transition period between A.D. 30 in A.D. 70. He was explaining to them that if they believe that Jesus had died and risen again from the dead, that God would bring with Jesus all those who had fallen asleep during this time. Then Paul includes some standing there in this text when he said, WE who are alive and remain until the coming of the Lord, will not precede those who have fallen asleep. In other words, something was going to change at the last trumpet.

Remember, the last trumpet sounded in Revelation chapter 11 immediately after the temple was destroyed. The temple was destroyed in A.D. 70. When Jesus spoke to Martha and said, "The hour is coming when all that are in the graves will hear the voice of the Son of Man and all they that hear will live", he was not referring to our day. He was referring to the last day of the old covenant. That day was not the last days of this age. It was the last days of the old covenant age. See Hebrews chapter 1. The writer the book of Hebrews called his day the last days when he said, God who in sundry times past spoke to us by the prophets hath in these last days spoken to us by his Son. He was talking about the last days of the old covenant age. Peter called his day the last days in Acts chapter 2 when he said, this is that which was spoken by the prophet Joel that in the last days I will pour out my Spirit on all flesh.

I am not asking you to believe everything I believe about end times. I am

119

just simply saying consider the possibility that much of what we thought was out in the distant future has been available to us all along. What was changing after the last trumpet is that we would no longer sleep. We would be changed in a moment, in the twinkling of an eye.

The Greek word he uses for "air" at the end of I Thessalonians chapter 4 when he says to them, we will be caught up together with them in the clouds to meet the Lord in the air, is a Greek word that means to breathe unconsciously, to respire or to blow air. It could literally be translated, the moment you take your last breath. There is a welcome meeting with the Lord into our eternal home. We pass from this life to the next with no interval to sleep. Perhaps the cloud is the great cloud of witnesses of Hebrews chapter 11. It is all our loved ones who have gone on before who are welcoming us home. It is those heroes of faith who have been cheering us on to the finish line.

This understanding helps me when I go to a funeral. I used to go to funerals and leave there utterly confused. The minister would say, "Grandma went home to be with the Lord". Those words would comfort me. But then he would get up to preach his sermon and would say, in that great getting up moment Grandma is going to go be with the Lord. Then we would get out at the graveyard and he would say, ashes to ashes and dust to dust. I am thinking in my mind, what have you done with Grandma? Is she with the Lord or is she waiting to get up or is she in the dust? I believe that the confusion comes when we do not understand his resurrection and we mix old covenant concepts concerning death, with new covenant concepts. For us who are beyond the A.D. 70 event, we no longer sleep. We are immediately in our eternal home the moment we take our last breath.

- Cloud Comings -

For a first-century Jew, cloud comings may have had a completely different meaning than our 21st century perception. They would have looked back to their Old Testament scriptures for its usage in other scriptures. Sometimes *coming in the clouds* meant a judgment on an apostate nation. Sometimes they spoke of the *glory cloud* in the Tabernacle of Moses. Hebrews chapter 11 spoke of the heroes of faith who were a great cloud of witnesses. Some places he talks about people being clouds without water, etc. Let us look at a few verses.

This Scripture talks about his coming in judgment upon the idols of Egypt.

19 The burden of Egypt. Behold, the Lord rideth upon a swift cloud, and shall come into Egypt: and the idols of Egypt shall be moved at his presence, and the heart of Egypt shall melt in the midst of it. Isa. 19:1 KJV

This Scripture talks about a coming in judgment upon Jerusalem.

13 Behold, he shall come up as clouds, and his chariots shall be as a whirlwind: his horses are swifter than eagles. Woe unto us! for we are spoiled. Jer. 4:13 KJV

The Scriptures teach us how God speaks in symbolic language and prophetic symbols.

11 He made darkness his secret place; his pavilion round about him were dark waters and thick clouds of the skies. Ps. 18:11 KJV

I could show you many more, but I want to show you one in the context of first century fulfillment.

*9 I beheld till the thrones were cast down, and the Ancient of days did sit, whose garment was white as snow, and the hair of his head like the pure wool: his throne was like the fiery flame, and his wheels as burning fire. 10 A fiery stream issued and came forth from before him: thousand thousands ministered unto him, and ten thousand times ten thousand stood before him: the judgment was set, **and the books were opened**. 11 I beheld then because of the voice of the great words which the horn spake: I beheld even till the beast was slain, and his body destroyed, and given to the burning flame. 12 As concerning the rest of the beasts, they had their dominion taken away: yet their lives were prolonged for a season and time. 13 I saw in the night visions, and, behold, one like **the Son of man*** *came with the clouds of heaven, and came to the Ancient of days, and they brought him near before him.* 14 And there was given him dominion, and glory, and a kingdom, that all people, nations, and languages, should serve him: his dominion is an everlasting dominion, which shall not pass away, and his kingdom that which shall not be destroyed. Dan. 7:9-14 KJV

The first thing I want you to notice is that the books were opened. These books were opened to judge all the old covenant Saints according to their works. For all of us beyond the resurrection, we are not judged according to our works. For those who are believers beyond the resurrection, there is no condemnation for those who are in Christ Jesus. The judgment of the wicked dead is a whole book itself and I do not have time to get into it here. However, I must note here that the Scripture tells us that we can have boldness in the day of judgment because as he is, so are we in this present world. His judgment was my judgment. Now the judgment is in my favor.

If you read the book of Daniel in the Amplified Bible, it will do all the historic work for you and it will become clear to you that this beast in the book is the Roman Empire. If you compare the beast in the book of Daniel with the beast in the book of Revelation, you will see they are the same beast.

40 And the fourth kingdom [Rome] shall be strong as iron, since iron breaks to pieces and subdues all things; and like iron which crushes, it shall break and crush all these. Dan. 2:40 AMP See also Dan. 7:7, 23.

If you read Daniel chapters 2 and 7 in the Amplified Bible, you will find that it tells you that in the days of these kings the God of Heaven would set up a Kingdom which would never be destroyed. The kingdom would not be left to other people. Jesus came on the scene in the days of the Roman Empire and his message was, repent, the Kingdom of Heaven is at hand.

When Jesus stands before the high priest and is judged, it is this quote from the book of Daniel that gets him crucified. All throughout the

Scripture Jesus refers to himself as the "Son of Man". When the high priest asked Jesus, tell us plainly are you the Christ, the Son of God. He called himself the Son of Man and then quoted Daniel 7:13&14, *"I saw in the night visions, and, behold, one like* **the Son of Man came with the clouds of heaven, and came to the ancient of days**, *and they brought him near before him. And there was given him dominion, and glory, and the kingdom, that all people, nations, and languages, should serve him: his dominion is an everlasting dominion, which shall not pass away, and his kingdom that which shall not be destroyed"*. He was given the Kingdom and dominion.

61 And said, This fellow said, **I am able to destroy the temple of God, and to build it in three days.** *62 And the high priest arose, and said unto him, Answerest thou nothing? what is it which these witness against thee? 63 But Jesus held his peace. And the high priest answered and said unto him, I adjure thee by the living God,* **that thou tell us whether thou be the Christ, the Son of God.** *64 Jesus saith unto him, Thou hast said: nevertheless I say unto you, Hereafter shall ye* **see the Son of man sitting on the right hand of power, and coming in the clouds of heaven.** *65 Then the high priest rent his clothes, saying, He hath spoken blasphemy; what further need have we of witnesses? behold, now ye have heard his blasphemy.* Matt. 26:61-65 KJV

The high priest rent his clothes and accused Jesus of blasphemy because he was identifying himself as King of the Jews, Messiah, and the Son of God; the one to whom dominion and glory and the Kingdom was given. This cloud was not to come and get us to take us to Heaven, it was him appearing before the ancient of days and receiving his coronation as King. The resurrection of Christ would signify that Israel's God had become king in the person of Jesus Christ. His victory over death would signify his ultimate dominion over every enemy, including death, the Roman Empire, the nation of Israel and over every creature. He was declared to be Lord by the resurrection of the dead. He was now Lord of the living and the dead. In the latter part of Daniel chapter 7 he declares that the Kingdom and the dominion and the greatness of the Kingdom under the whole

Heaven would be given to the people of the Saints of the Most High. We are included in that dominion and we now rule and reign with him in the earth as a kingdom of priests.

- Back to the Garden -

When God drove them out of the garden, he placed at the East of the Garden of Eden cherubim and a flaming sword which turned every way to *keep the way of the tree of life*. I want you to notice he did not put them there to keep you out of the garden. He put them there to keep the way of the tree of life.

In John chapter 20, there is another garden. It is the place of Jesus' sepulcher. When Mary came to the tomb, she saw a repeat of what happened with Lazarus. The stone was rolled away. When Mary stooped down to look into the sepulcher, she saw two Angels in white. One was at the head and the other at the feet where the body of Jesus had lain. If you have ever seen a picture of the Mercy Seat in the Tabernacle of Moses, you will remember that it had two cherubim on the Mercy Seat. They turn to face each other with their wings outstretched over the Mercy Seat of the Ark of the Covenant of the Lord.

Remember, the Old Testament is Jesus concealed. The New Testament is Jesus revealed. The Mercy Seat in the Tabernacle of Moses was a shadow of what was happening in the tomb of Jesus with an Angel standing at the head and an Angel standing at the foot where he had lain. It is an incredible picture of the real Mercy Seat because Jesus is called our propitiation for sin. The Greek word for propitiation means *a mercy seat*. They had just found the real Ark of the Covenant of the Lord. They had just found the real Mercy Seat. The judgment seat was now a Mercy Seat. But I think they also found the two Angels that were pointing the way back to the tree of life, back into the Paradise of God. Remember, they were not there to keep you out. They were there to keep the way of the tree of life.

The sword that turned every way in the garden of Eden is found in

Hebrews chapter 4 when he is talking about the *rest* of God. He said, for the word of God is life-giving, powerful, sharper than any two-edged sword. The two-edged sword in the book of Hebrews is in the context of *rest*. It is not just any word that is life-giving. It is the word that flows from *rest*. That same chapter points us to a faithful High Priest on a Mercy Seat. It points us to the one who is our Mercy Seat. It is the place where we can come boldly to the throne of grace, obtain mercy, and find grace to help in the time of need.

I do not think it is an accident that everything that Jesus did in his redemptive work, he did in a garden. I have already written much about this in other chapters, so I will not repeat myself here except to say. when Jesus was on the cross there were two thieves that hung beside him. One of them represented the serpent who questioned his identity just like the first Adam. He said to him if you be the son of God save yourself and us. Does that remind you of the voice of the serpent? The other thief represented the entire Adam family. That thief said to Jesus, we are getting what we deserve, but this man has done nothing worthy of death. You see, you got everything you deserved 2000 years ago when you were crucified with Christ. He then said to Jesus, remember me when you come into your kingdom. This word *remember* is the same word I spoke of in an earlier chapter that could possibly mean *put me back together again*. RE-member me. Jesus said to this thief, this day you will be with me in Paradise. The Greek word for Paradise in this text could be translated Eden. When Mary stooped down to look into the tomb of Jesus, she had just found the gate to Paradise, the way back into the garden of God, into his finished work. What these Angels with their outstretched wings were pointing to is, "this is the way, walk ye in it.". The death, burial and resurrection of Jesus is what would roll the stone away to give access to a Mercy Seat. It was the way back into Paradise. Jesus appeared to Mary in the garden and she supposed him to be the gardener. He in fact was the gardener and he had just put them back in a finished work. Now he would guard and keep this garden.

- The Rich Man and Lazarus -

In Luke chapter 16 beginning in verse 19 is the story of the rich man and Lazarus. The rich man in the story represents the nation of Israel who were clothed in purple and fine linen and fared sumptuously every day. They had the covenants of promise and they were the natural seed of Abraham. They thought they were rich and increased in goods and had need of nothing. They did not know they were wretched, miserable, poor, and blind. They were the ones that Jesus was talking to in Matthew chapter 5 when he said, you are blessed when you are poor in spirit. That does not mean you go around with your head hanging down and depressed. It means that moving from an old covenant paradigm requires you to recognize the spiritual deficit you were in under the old covenant. It requires you to recognize your need for God. Jesus told them, you are blessed when you are hungry and thirsty for righteousness. Remember, he is speaking to an audience who thinks they are already righteous based on the old covenant. Perhaps when Jesus said, it is hard for a rich man to enter the Kingdom, he was not talking about how much money you have. Perhaps he was talking about recognizing your need of him.

Lazarus in this story represents the Gentiles. The name Lazarus is the Greek equivalent of the Hebrew name Eleazar, who was the Gentile servant of Abraham that was going to receive the inheritance. He represented the Gentiles because even the dogs eat the crumbs that fall from the master's table. Jesus used that terminology when he addressed the Gentile woman who needed healing for her daughter. He told her in Matthew 15:24, I am sent to the lost sheep of the house of Israel. In other words, it was to the Jew first and then to the Gentile. He then told her, it is not proper to take the children's bread and give it to the dogs. She said, even the dogs eat the crumbs which fall from the master's table. Her faith accessed a miracle that was not yet available to her.

In the parable of the rich man and Lazarus, Lazarus died and was carried into the bosom of Abraham. When the rich man died, he was in hell and lifted up his eyes, being in torment, and saw Abraham afar off and Lazarus in his bosom. He cried out, Father Abraham, have mercy on me and send Lazarus that he may dip the tip of his finger in water and cool my tongue for I am tormented in this flame. In this story Abraham responds to his request and calls him a son. He was the natural seed of Abraham and spoke of the nation of Israel, which was about to lose their inheritance to the Gentiles.

The rich man asked Father Abraham to send Lazarus to testify to his brother so that he would not be sent to this awful place of torment. Abraham said to the rich man, they have Moses and the prophets, let them hear them. The rich man said to him, "Nay, Father Abraham: but if one went unto them from the dead, they will repent". Father Abraham said unto him, if they hear not Moses and the prophets, neither will they be persuaded, though one rose from the dead. I believe this parable is connected to Lazarus who was raised from the dead by Jesus. Jesus fulfilled their request to send one from the dead to warn the nation of Israel not to come to this place of torment, even though they had been warned continuously by Moses and the prophets. I promise you the moment Jesus raised Lazarus from the dead, they told the scribes and Pharisees. They probably said, who told them these things, please tell us his name is not Lazarus. Because even though one rose from the dead, still they did not believe. He did not just raise someone random from the dead, he raised a man by the name of Lazarus. The kingdom was about to be taken from them and given to a nation producing the fruit thereof.

In Bullinger's notes in the Companion Bible, he tells us that there is a great gulf that is fixed between the two worlds. This word *gulf* in the Greek language is a medical term that means *a gaping wound.* I submit to you the gaping wound was inflicted on Calvary and there is only one way into the covenants of promise, through faith in his finished work. But still they did not believe that Jesus was the Christ, the Son of the living God, so that believing they could have life through his name. They did not believe even though one rose from the dead. Jesus did not say, one of these days I am going to be the resurrection and the life. He said, "I AM" the resurrection and the life. If you believe it, then roll the stone away. Remove the grave clothes, loose them and let them go.

CHAPTER 8
I AM THE WAY THE TRUTH AND THE LIFE

6 *Jesus saith unto him, I am the way, the truth, and the life: no man cometh unto the Father, but by me.* John 14:6 KJV

Before we get into the meat of this verse let me set the context once again. The disciples have gathered in an upper room to keep the feast of Passover. It was the final Passover of the old covenant. Jesus said to them, with great desire have I desired to keep this Passover with you. Jesus knew that he would be the fulfillment of the feast of Passover and that after this Passover they would never again have to kill another Lamb. He would show them at the covenant table that this is the end of the old covenant and the beginning of the new covenant. The death of the Lamb of God in this final Passover would be the beginning of a brand-new Exodus out of the slavery of an Egyptian religious system. No longer would they experience the whips and chains of the taskmasters of religion. He was about to deliver them into the glorious liberty of sonship.

He washed the feet of the disciples to demonstrate to them that in this new Kingdom that the greatest of them would be able to humble themselves and serve others. In this new covenant we are not servants who are trying to become sons. We are sons who desire to serve. He was demonstrating to them that ministry is not about a title. It is about a towel. He was demonstrating to them that the Kingdom of God does not function like the kingdoms of men. It does not function from a hierarchical system. It functions from sons that have a heart to serve creation.

As Jesus served the Passover meal, he raised his cup and said, this cup is the new covenant in my blood. I will not drink wine again until I drink it new with you in my Father's kingdom. In acts chapter 2 on the day of Pentecost, he popped the cork on a vintage of new wine that had never been drunk before and toasted the coming of the Kingdom. Remember,

128

the Kingdom of God is not meat and drink. It is righteousness, peace and joy located in the Holy Ghost.

Please note that you cannot put new wine into an old wine skin. That does not mean you cannot sing charismatic songs in a Presbyterian Church. It means you cannot put the new wine of the new covenant into the old wine skin of old covenant thinking. Most church splits I am aware of have come as a result of trying to mix the two covenants. They will not mix. It will break the old wine skin and the wine will run out. Paul calls the mixture of law and grace a perversion of the gospel. We cannot preach the parts of law that fit our culture and call that the gospel. We must truly become able ministers of the new covenant, not of the letter that kills but of the spirit that gives life.

In this final Last Supper Jesus took the bread and gave it even to his betrayer. Remember, everyone at the table, save John, would leave Jesus before the night was over. Peter would deny him three times. I believe Peter truly meant it when he said to Jesus, I will lay down my life for your sake. Jesus answered him, will you lay down your life for my sake? Truly, truly I say to you, the rooster shall not crow until you have denied me three times.

- The Rooster Has Something to Say -

As the events of this fateful night unfold, the words of Jesus would come to pass with incredible accuracy. Peter's third denial at the fireside with a young damsel within earshot, he would curse and say, I know him not. At that moment, the rooster crowed. Now what we normally preach is that the rooster crowed to rat Peter out. But if you have ever lived on a farm you know that the rooster always crows to announce a new day. Perhaps the rooster did *not* crow to rat Peter out. Perhaps he crowed to announce a new day was on the scene. Peter with his best efforts had failed the Lord. Remember, he was under an old covenant and at this point was not filled with the Spirit. It was through human willpower that he was operating. But even his best intentions had failed. I want to announce to you a new day. What you could not do in your own human strength

129

without the indwelling Holy Spirit, you will now find possible as you embrace the supply of the Spirit in this new day.

Most of the time when we read the Scriptures we come to the end of the chapter and we think that is the end of the story. However, in the original language, they did not have chapters and verses. So, I want to show you two verses that I do not believe are separated. I believe they are still part of the ongoing conversation. The last verse of John chapter 13 and the first verse of John chapter 14 are connected.

38 Jesus answered him, Wilt thou lay down thy life for my sake? Verily, verily, I say unto thee, The cock shall not crow, till thou hast denied me thrice. 1 Let not your heart be troubled: ye believe in God, believe also in me. John 13:38-14:1 KJV

When you read these verses in context, they bring new meaning to what was happening. Jesus said to Peter, you are going to deny me before the rooster crows, but do not let your heart be troubled! Do you see it? Do not let your heart be troubled even when you fail. Under the old covenant, failure was inevitable. You did not have the indwelling Holy Spirit, the helper to do in you what you could not do in your own human strength. His instruction to Peter was, in the moment of your failure do not let your heart be troubled. If you believe in God, believe also in me. It is in this context that he said, I am the way, the truth, and the life; no man cometh unto the father, but by me. Notice he did not say I am the way to heaven. He said, I am the way to the Father's house. The life of the coming age is a life lived in the context of sonship, living out a father-son relationship. I have written much about this in prior chapters. Let us look at these verses.

*4 Let not your heart be troubled: ye believe in God, believe also in me. 2 In my Father's house are many mansions: if it were not so, I would have told you. I go to prepare a place for you. 3 And if I go and prepare a place for you, I will come again, and receive you unto myself; **that where I am, there ye may be also.** 4 And whither I go ye know, and the way ye know. 5 Thomas saith unto him, Lord, we know not whither thou goest; and how* *can we know the way? 6 Jesus saith unto him, **I am the way, the truth, and the life**: no man cometh unto the Father, but by me.* John 14:1-6 KJV

I want to draw your attention in these texts to the words "I am". He said to them, I go to prepare a place for you, and I will come again and receive you unto myself that where I am you may be also. The question I would ask you to consider is, where was he? And where was he going?

First, he was going to the Father, and told them that no one can come to the Father except through him.

*8 Philip saith unto him, Lord, shew us the Father, and it sufficeth us. 9 Jesus saith unto him, Have I been so long time with you, and yet hast thou not known me, Philip? he that hath seen me hath seen the Father; and how sayest thou then, Shew us the Father? 10 Believest thou not **that I am in the Father, and the Father in me**? the words that I speak unto you I speak not of myself: but the Father that dwelleth in me, he doeth the works. 11 Believe me that **I am in the Father, and the Father in me**: or else believe me for the very works' sake. 12 Verily, verily, I say unto you, He that believeth on me, the works that I do shall he do also; and greater works than these shall he do; because I go unto my Father. 13 And whatsoever ye shall ask in my name, that will I do, that the Father may be glorified in the Son. 14 If ye shall ask any thing in my name, I will do it. 15 If ye love me, keep my commandments. 16 And I will pray the Father, and he shall give you another Comforter, that he may abide with you for ever; 17 Even the Spirit of truth; whom the world cannot receive, because it seeth him not, neither knoweth him: but ye know him; for he dwelleth with you, and shall be in you. 18 I will not leave you comfortless: I will come to you. 19 Yet a little while, and the world seeth me no more; but ye see me: because I live, ye shall live also. 20 At that day ye shall know that **I am in my Father, and ye in me, and I in you.*** John 14:8-20 KJV

Do you see it? I go to prepare a place for you that where I am you may be also. Where is he? He is in the Father and the Father is in him. Where he is taking us is into the Father. He was also telling them that just like he is in the Father and the Father is in him, he and the Father will come and take up their abode within us.

*23 Jesus answered and said unto him, If a man love me, he will keep my words: and my Father will love him, and we will come unto him, and **make our abode** with him.* John 14:23 KJV

What I want to point out to you in this chapter is that in verse 2 it says, in my Father's house are many mansions. Most of the time our mind goes to a location in Heaven where we think God is building me a house. And as soon as he gets my house ready, he will come and get me. Most people think he has been working on this house for over 2000 years and it is still not ready. In reality it only took him seven days to create the entire universe. Consider the possibility that something much bigger is being said here. Let me preface what I am about to say by telling you that I think Heaven will be much more glorious than just getting a big house to live in all by yourself when you die. I am not taking Heaven from you. I am just saying that this verse is not a description of Heaven.

Consider the possibility that this house is not just for you to live in. It is for the Father to live in. As a matter of fact, this Greek word for *mansion* is only used one other place in the Scriptures. It is used in the verse I just printed above and is translated as *abode*. The word mansion and the word abode are the exact same Greek word. It is the usage of this word in verse 23 that makes it clear to me about this house. God's house is us. We are his many membered body with Jesus being the head. In other words, we are the house in which God lives. We are his mansion and in my Father's house is his many membered body. There are many mansions, many dwelling places. He lives in us and we live in him. We are his house and he is our dwelling place. Remember when I shared with you the verse in Revelation chapter 21? The Message Bible says, look, God has moved into the neighborhood. He is made his home in men. God finally realized his dream when he said, let them build me a house that I may dwell among them. The desire that God had from the beginning was to *tabernacle* himself not just among us, but in us. I am in him, and he is in me. He is my house and I am his house.

132

The place he was preparing for us was an adoption into his family that could only come through his death, burial, and resurrection. It was in this context that he said, I will not leave you comfortless. The Greek word for *comfortless* in this text is the Greek word for *orphan*. It could literally be translated *I will not leave you orphans*. I will not leave you fatherless. The mission of Jesus was to show us the Father, to bring us into intimate relationship with him. Do you realize what a revolutionary concept of this must have been to a first-century Israelite? When Jesus declared, I and my Father are one, they picked up stones in which to stone him. Jesus said to them, many good works I have shown you from my Father. For which one of these works do you stone me? They responded, "for a good work we stone thee not, but because thou being a man makest thyself God". Jesus was not a man who made himself God. He was God who made himself man. He was identifying with God as his Father. The apostle John included us in this union when he declared, behold what an incredible quality of love the Father has bestowed upon us that we might be called the sons of God. He introduced the concept of God being Abba Father. He came to show us God in a different light; not the austere old man on a Victorian chair with a club in his hand ready to hit us upside the head. He showed us a loving, caring Father who is only interested in seeing us live the life he intended for us.

27 Jesus resumed talking to the people, but now tenderly. "The Father has given me all these things to do and say. **This is a unique Father-Son operation, coming out of Father and Son intimacies and knowledge.** *No one knows the Son the way the Father does, nor the Father the way the Son does.* **But I'm not keeping it to myself; I'm ready to go over it line by line with anyone willing to listen.** *28 "Are you tired? Worn out? Burned out on religion?* **Come to me. Get away with me and you'll recover your life.** *I'll show you how to take a real rest. 29 Walk with me and work with me — watch how I do it. Learn the unforced rhythms of grace. I won't lay anything heavy or ill-fitting on you. 30 Keep company with me and you'll learn to live freely and lightly."* Matt. 11:27-30 MSG

4 Now I say, That the heir, as long as he is a child, differeth nothing from a

servant, though he be lord of all; 2 But is under tutors and governors until the time appointed of the father. 3 Even so we, when we were children, were in bondage under the elements of the world: 4 But when the fulness of the time was come, God sent forth his Son, made of a woman, made under the law, 5 **To redeem them that were under the law, that we might receive the adoption of sons. 6 And because ye are sons, God hath sent forth the Spirit of his Son into your hearts, crying, Abba, Father.** *7* **Wherefore thou art no more a servant, but a son; and if a son, then an heir of God through Christ.** Gal. 4:1-7 KJV

Do you see it? As long as they were under the law, they were under the governors and tutors and the bondage of the elements of the old covenant. We are no longer orphans and have been adopted and placed into the family of God. We are no longer servants, but sons. God has sent forth the Spirit of his Son into our hearts and now we cry Abba. Abba is a term of endearment. It is like our term in the English language for daddy.

Jesus said in John chapter14, I will not leave you orphans. I will come to you. He also said in this chapter, it is expedient for you that I go away, because if I do not go away the comforter will not come. In other words, if I remain with you in physical form there will be no indwelling Holy Ghost. But if I go, I will pray to the Father, and he will give you another comforter, that he may abide with you forever. What a divine house party; the Father, Son and Holy Ghost living and dwelling inside us. This text finds its fulfillment in Acts chapters 1 and 2 with the outpouring of the Holy Ghost. He was taken up and a cloud received him out of their sight. In the next chapter the Holy Ghost is poured out. Yes, he went away in Acts chapter 1. But in Acts chapter 2 he came again and received us unto himself, that where he is, we may be also. We are now in him and he is in us.

Now I am sure that if you read the whole of John chapter 14 you will see that Jesus said to them if you love me keep my commandments. Some would say, see there, he is taking us back under the law. I reply, this is not a commandment from the law of Moses. This was the new commandment he gave in John chapter 13 when he said, a new commandment I give you that you love one another. If you love one another your behavior toward each other changes. You will not steal, kill, or do anything that is unlike Jesus. You now have the love of God shed abroad in your heart by way of the Holy Ghost that empowers you to love.

When Jesus told Peter let not your heart be troubled, even after he had betrayed the Lord, I think he was saying to him, Peter, I know that you will do the best you can with your human strength. But even in your best strength you are going to fail. He also said, I am not going to leave you powerless. I am going to fill you with the Holy Ghost, and it will enable you to do what you could not do with your own human strength. You will deliver with boldness on the day of Pentecost the message that will bring 3000 people into the church in one day. I think it is worth mentioning that Peter denied the Lord three times. But when Jesus appears to Peter after his resurrection, he asked him three times, "Peter, do you love me"? He gives Peter the opportunity to tell him three times how much he loves him. In other words, he denied him three times. But he also got to tell him "I love you" three times. I am glad that our God is a God of the second chance, a third chance and on and on.

- The Comforter -

There are two words I want to draw your attention to in John chapter 14. Those two words are *comfortless* and *comforter*. We have already dealt with the word comfortless, which is a Greek word that means I will not leave you orphans. The second word comforter is a completely different word in the Greek language. It is the Greek word *paraclete*. The word paraclete means to be your advocate, your legal assistant for defense, one who gives aid, one who pleads another's cause, etc. In other words, the comforter is your advocate. I want you to notice he is not the prosecuting attorney he is defense counsel. There is one that accuses you, even Moses, whom you serve. But the Holy Spirit is not the accuser of the brethren. You have an attorney on retainer. His name is Jesus Christ the righteous, and he ever lives to make intercession for you. Let us look at the work of the Holy Spirit in this verse.

26 But when the Comforter is come, whom I will send unto you from the

*Father, even the Spirit of truth, which proceedeth from the Father, **he shall testify of me***: John 15:26 KJV

The work of the Holy Spirit in the life of the believer is to testify of Jesus to bring to your remembrance all things that he has spoken to you. The Holy Spirit can only testify to what is truth. The Holy Spirit continually reminds us of the person and work of Jesus Christ.

7 Nevertheless I tell you the truth; It is expedient for you that I go away: for if I go not away, the Comforter will not come unto you; but if I depart, I will send him unto you. 8 And when he is come, he will reprove the world of sin, and of righteousness, and of judgment: 9 Of sin, because they believe not on me; 10 Of righteousness, because I go to my Father, and ye see me no more; 11 Of judgment, because the prince of this world is judged. 12 I have yet many things to say unto you, but ye cannot bear them now. 13 Howbeit when he, the Spirit of truth, is come, he will guide you into all truth: for he shall not speak of himself; but whatsoever he shall hear, that shall he speak: and he will shew you things to come. John 16:7-13 KJV

In the above two Scriptures, the word *comforter* is the Greek word *paraclete*. There are three dimensions of the work of the Holy Spirit in this Scripture.

1. To reprove the world of sin, because they believe not

When you are an unbeliever, the Holy Spirit broods over you to convince and convict you of the truth that you need a Savior. His goal is to make a believer out of unbelievers. He does that by testifying of the truth.

2. To convince and convict you of righteousness

As believers, the Holy Spirit does not convict you of sin. He convicts and convinces us of righteousness. I am praying that God will release the spirit of conviction upon his people in this hour to convict them of righteousness. Remember, your Paraclete your Advocate can only testify of what is truth. The truth is you are the

136

righteousness of God in Christ Jesus. An incredible exchange took place in his redemptive work. He that knew no sin was made to be sin for us that we might be made the righteousness of God. He did absolutely nothing wrong to be made sin for me. I did absolutely nothing right to be made righteous. It was completely based on his free gift. Because of the abundance of grace and the gift of righteousness, we reign in life by one Christ Jesus. Righteousness is a gift. You did not earn it. It was given to you freely. Now the Holy Spirit is convicting you of that truth.

This reminds me of the popular song that is out right now By Lauren Daigle that says, *"You say I am loved when I can't feel a thing. You say I am strong, when I think I am weak. You say I am held when I am falling short. And when I don't belong, oh You say I am yours, and I believe, oh I believe what you say of me. I believe."* In other words, you may call yourself a sinner. However, the Holy Spirit in you cannot agree with that. He can only testify of what is true of you. He can only testify of Jesus and his work and what he has made you to be in the new creation. That is all with which he can come into agreement. You may say I am sick, but your advocate the Holy Spirit says, by his stripes you were healed. You may say I am not a son of God, but your advocate says. I can only testify about what is true of you. The truth is you are still a son, even if you are a son in a hog pen. The moment the prodigal son remembered who his father was, he left the hog pen.

The conviction of righteousness will change your behavior far more than the conviction of sin. When you truly become convicted of righteousness you will act like you are righteous. The just will live by faith. What you really believe, is what you will act on. When we constantly remind people of their failures, we are reinforcing a false identity. But the Holy Spirit only comes into agreement with truth. If any two or three of you agree on earth as touching any one thing, it will be established. When we come into agreement with the Father, Son and Holy Spirit, something happens in the realm of manifestation. The Holy Spirit will not let you believe a lie about yourself. He will convict you of righteousness.

3. To convince and convict you of judgment

> The Prince of this world has already judged. Your defense counsel will convince you that as a believer your judgment is not in your future. It is in your past. When he was lifted up, he drew all judgment into himself so that you can have boldness in the day of judgment. As he is, so are we in this present world. That is the only thing in which your Attorney, your Advocate, can come into agreement. The only thing the Paraclete will tell you is that Adam is dead, the devil is defeated, and Jesus is Lord!

Many years ago, I wrote a play for a youth camp called **The Advocate**. This youth camp was set up like a courtroom. We had someone dressed in black like the prosecuting attorney. He was the accuser of the brethren. My brother played God in the play and I played Jesus the advocate.

When the prosecuting attorney, the accuser of the brethren came in the room, we had a scene where a news reporter was interviewing the prosecuting attorney. The prosecutor said to the news reporter, "This is an open and shut case. I have the letter of the law on my side. I am going to throw the book at the accused." Sometimes I wonder who these ministries work for when they stand in the pulpit every week and throw the book at us. They preach the letter of the law and tell us how bad we are. They use the letter of the law with which to do it.

When I walked in the room playing Jesus as the advocate the news reporter said to me, "It looks like an open and shut case, and your adversary has the letter of the law on his side". I replied, "He is trying my client on an antiquated law. He is not abreast of the new legislation".

The gavel dropped and court was in session. God the Father looked at my client and he said to him, "Would you like to enter a plea"? I said to my client, "Stand up and tell him, yes, I would like to enter a plea. I would like to plead the blood of Jesus" and then sit back down. Then the judge asked my client, "Would you like to make a confession?" I said to my client, "Stand up and tell him, yes, I would like to confess with my mouth the Lord Jesus and tell you that I believe God raised him from the dead." As the court case proceeded, I had the prosecutor bring out many laws from the law of Moses. Everything from it is illegal under the law of Moses. To touch a pig means you cannot eat pork chops, bacon, or sausage. He brought out passages like, do not mingle your thread in a garment with different kinds of thread. He spoke of laws that I knew no one in the room was keeping. We do pick and choose the parts of the law that fit our culture and call that the gospel. It is not the gospel at all. It is a mixture. Once the prosecutor was done with all his accusations. I lifted my hand and said, "Father, may I approach the bench?" The Father said, "Yes, son, you ever live to litigate. You ever live to make intercession."

I said to God the judge of all, "My client may look like Bob Smith, in Adam. *(You can put your own name in that spot if you want.)* But a simple DNA test will prove that my client is not Bob Smith, in Adam. My client is Bob Smith, in Christ. My client has been *re-gene-erated*. He has been *re-gened*. As a matter of fact, my client is the long-lost son of God, the Father himself. His new birth gave him a new DNA." I entered exhibit A, a baptismal certificate and said to the judge, "Bob Smith, in Adam, was buried in a watery grave. My client may look like Bob Smith, in Adam. But my client is Bob Smith, in Christ. Even if you find him guilty, I have already suffered the death penalty on his behalf. I have a pardon signed in blood. And if the glove does not fit, you must acquit."

The gavel dropped and God the judge said, "Bob Smith has been declared not guilty in the highest court of the universe. There is therefore now no condemnation to those who are in Christ Jesus." The bailiff left the platform, came down and unlocked the shackles that were on my client. When he did, the youth camp went crazy. It took me 15 minutes to regain control of the crowd. Once the crowd was calm, I lifted my hand one more time and said to God the judge, "Father, may I approach the bench." I then proceeded to say to the judge, "Since we won the criminal charge and we proved in court that my client was Your Honor long-lost Son, we would like to enter into a civil case with the court. We would like to ask for the inheritance that belongs to my client." I raised my Bible and said, "I have a copy of my Father's last will and testament." You see, even in the courtrooms of the United States the term *prayer* is a legal term. When a lawyer ends a court case., often they will say, these things we pray the court. Every time we pray, we make a legal motion. It is a petition. It is our legal right because of the will. Our attorney will make sure we get our inheritance. Do not settle out of court. We are heirs and joint heirs with Jesus Christ. Aren't you glad you have an attorney, a Paraclete who has never lost a case?

He in fact is **the way, the truth, and the life**. He is the way to the Father, and he will not leave us orphans. He will not leave us without an attorney. He will not leave us, comfortless.

CHAPTER 9
I AM THE TRUE VINE

*15 **I am the true vine**, and my Father is the husbandman. 2 Every branch in me that beareth not fruit he taketh away: and every branch that beareth fruit, he purgeth it, that it may bring forth more fruit. 3 Now ye are clean through the word which I have spoken unto you. 4 Abide in me, and I in you. As the branch cannot bear fruit of itself, except it abide in the vine; no more can ye, except ye abide in me. 5 I am the vine, ye are the branches: He that abideth in me, and I in him, the same bringeth forth much fruit: for without me ye can do nothing. 6 If a man abide not in me, he is cast forth as a branch, and is withered; and men gather them, and cast them into the fire, and they are burned. 7 If ye abide in me, and my words abide in you, ye shall ask what ye will, and it shall be done unto you.* John 15:1-7 KJV

Once again, context is everything. The seventh time that Jesus says, "I Am", follows the concepts that we discussed in the prior chapter. If we abide in him and he abides in us, then we are connected to the true vine.

20 At that day ye shall know that I am in my Father, and ye in me, and I in you. John 14:20 KJV

He makes clear in John chapters 14 and 15 that the new commandment is to **love one another**. Love is the result of our union with him because God is love. Love is not something you fake or manufacture. It is a fruit. It is a result of being connected to the right root. I want to emphasize that this is not the old commandment from the law of Moses. This is a brand-new commandment. Jesus made the statement throughout the Scriptures if you love me keep my commandments. He is not talking about the law of Moses.

Have you ever been to someone's home for dinner and they had a beautiful centerpiece on the table that looked like fresh fruit? It was so beautiful that you thought, I will have one of those beautiful peaches. But to bite into it you found out it was plastic with peach fuzz. Religion is much like that centerpiece on the table. It looks good on Sunday and it almost looks real. However, when you bite into it, it has no substance. I personally would rather have vine-ripe fruit that had a blemish or a bug bite in it than I would to eat fake fruit.

Have you ever walked out into your yard and looked at your apple or peach tree and then stood there and preached to it, demanding it to grow fruit? Of course, you have not. Someone would think you have lost your mind. I am afraid that is what we have made of our church services. Preachers stand in pulpits and yell at fruit trees trying to get them to produce fruit. You can pressure them and threatened them all you want, but fruit is not a result of being threatened. You can get people to act like they are bearing fruit, only to find out it is fake. They may pretend like they love you or their neighbor. They may even say to your face, I love you brother. Although, in fact they are thinking, I hope you fall and break your neck on the way out of here. Love is not something that you manufacture. Love is a result of being connected to him who is love. The Scripture clearly says, "God is love". I love him because he first loved me. He initiated something that created a response. It is like receiving a love note when you were an adolescent. Someone wrote a note saying, I love you. Do you love me? Check *yes* or *no*. When you received that note you may have not been aware that person even had feelings for you. It may have awakened a response in you, *wow, I am loved*. Then you checked the *yes* box and a relationship began.

I genuinely believe that the gospel is just such a message to the world, for God *so* loved the world! He will keep on loving the world until there is a response. Love never fails. His love is relentless. As a matter of fact, I think sometimes God is a stalker. He will never leave you or give up on you. He is like Forest Gump. He will take you back when all you have is one dying breath and your body is racked with pain, because *stupid is what stupid does*. But you could have had an entire life filled with the unconditional love of God.

When you truly fall in love with him all your service will flow from that love. You will no longer serve because you *must*. You will serve because you *want to*. Love is a powerful force. It will make you drive through a snowstorm or get on an airplane in the middle of the night to go see the one you love. It will make you spend money you do not have, etc. That reminds me of the song, "The Things We Do for Love". You may not have much material wealth or possessions, but if you have love you are a wealthy person.

I am convinced that when people truly meet this God of love, they will not have to be coerced to go to church, give offerings or do the things that please him. They will not do it because they must. They will do it because they choose. I think the reason people hesitate to go to church, give in offerings or serve in any capacity is because of the abuses they have encountered.

I believe God has been so misrepresented that when you mentioned him, they cringe. Their concept of God is so warped by religion. One of the Old Testament prophets said, when you see him, there is no beauty that you would desire him. He also declared Jesus was wounded in the house of his friends. I think these portions of Scripture speak of his crucifixion. You could also apply them to the fact that religion has so misrepresented him that there is no beauty that is attractive to people. However, the writer of the Song of Solomon said, he is altogether lovely. I want to present a God who is altogether lovely so that my passionate description of him creates the same response as the woman in the Song of Solomon. When the daughters of Jerusalem heard her describe him from the top of his head to the soles of his feet they said, where is your beloved, that we may seek him with thee? The more I have discovered how he truly is, the more I fall in love with him.

- The Fruit of the Spirit -

Let us look at the text in Galatians chapter 5 where it speaks of the fruit of the spirit. The first thing I want to point out to you is what it means to be in the flesh. I am not saying it is exclusive to this, but at least one aspect of being in the flesh means *to be under the law.*

*3 Are ye so foolish? having begun in the Spirit, **are ye now made perfect by the flesh?*** Gal. 3:3 KJV

*5 For **when we were in the flesh, the motions of sins, which were by the law,** did work in our members to bring forth fruit unto death. 6 But now we are delivered from the law, that being dead wherein we were held; that we should serve in newness of spirit, and not in the oldness of the letter.* Rom. 7:5-6 KJV

The entire seventh chapter of Romans Paul spoke about the difference between being under law and being under grace. At the end of that chapter he said, for the good that I desire to do, I do not do; but the evil that I do not want to do, that I practice. It is the roller coaster ride of religion. I was raised to believe most of my life that this is the plight of the Christian walk. Then I discovered that this is not the plight, but the result of being under the law. It is the result of being in the flesh. Trying to live through human effort and strength and what your flesh can produce to please God. Then you find out you are up and down; you have the victory and then you do not have the victory. You sit around thinking: *He loves me, he loves me not he loves me, he loves me not.* Sadly, so many are still on this roller coaster ride. It was in his desperation that the apostle Paul cried out, "Who shall deliver me from the body of this death?" The resounding answer is, ***Thank God, he will!***

As we look at the context of Galatians chapter 5, where he talks about the fruit of the spirit, he first warns the Galatian church to stand fast in the liberty wherewith Christ has made us free and be not entangled again with the yoke of bondage. That yoke of bondage was the bondage of legalism and being under the law. Paul went on to tell them that if they are circumcised, Christ will profit them nothing. He told them that if they go back to circumcision that they are in debt to do the whole law, and then Christ will become of none effect to them. It is in that context that he said to them, if you seek to be justified by the law, you have fallen from grace. To fall from grace does not mean you sinned Saturday night. Falling from grace means you have gone back to trying to be justified by the law. Paul told the Galatian church that neither circumcision nor uncircumcision

144

avails anything, but faith that works by love. He warned them not to mix law and grace because a little leaven leavens the whole lump. He told them if you are led by the Spirit you are not under the law. But if you are under the law and you are trying to please God human strength, you are in the flesh. Here are the results of being in the flesh.

*18 But if ye be led of the Spirit, ye are not under the law. 19 **Now the works of the flesh are manifest**, which are these; Adultery, fornication, uncleanness, lasciviousness, 20 Idolatry, witchcraft, hatred, variance, emulations, wrath, strife, seditions, heresies, 21 Envyings, murders, drunkenness, revellings, and such like: of the which I tell you before, as I have also told you in time past, that they which do such things shall not inherit the kingdom of God. 22 But the fruit of the Spirit is love, joy, peace, longsuffering, gentleness, goodness, faith, 23 Meekness, temperance: against such there is no law. 24 And they that are Christ's have crucified the flesh with the affections and lusts. 25 If we live in the Spirit, let us also walk in the Spirit. 26 Let us not be desirous of vain glory, provoking one another, envying one another.*

Gal. 5:18-26 KJV

Do you see it? If you are in the flesh, that is if you are under the law, this is the result: adultery, fornication, hatred, variance, strife, sedition, etc. This is the stuff you see in every church. You see a lot of that *plastic fruit* I talked about earlier. It looks good on a table, but it has no substance to it. The exact opposite is the result of being in the Spirit, connected to the true vine. Connected to the true root will produce in you the fruit of the spirit. It will produce love, joy, peace, long-suffering, etc. I found that once I discovered the gospel of grace that the fruit of the Spirit began to appear in my life effortlessly. Because I understood how God views me, I can view my neighbor in the same light. Without all the holier-than-thou looks or thinking about others like "I thank God I am not like that sinner", I found that I genuinely love people. I do not love them because I must, but because I want to!

We will become what we behold. If we see God as an angry, condemning tyrant, we will act the same. But I say to you that is idolatry. That is not being a true representative of God's image in the earth. If you want to know what God is like, look at Jesus. He is the express image of the Father. No wonder Paul cried out, "Oh, that I might know him."

- You Thought Israel Was the True Vine -

Since Jesus is the true vine and we are the branches we must see who they thought was the true vine. We will explore what branches are removed. Remember, every chapter that I have written was a comparison between old covenant and new covenant. For instance, you thought the manna that fell in the wilderness in the Old Testament was the bread. But that was not the bread. *I Am* is the true bread. You thought the door into the sheepfold was through the straight and narrow. That is performance-based Christianity. But that is not the door. Jesus said, *I am the door.* You thought the true shepherds were the corrupt shepherds of Israel. But they are not the shepherds at all. The Shepherd Jesus said, *I am the good Shepherd.* In this chapter I will show you the truth. You thought Israel was the vine, but that vine and that branch was about to be cut down and cast into the fire. This casting into the fire happened in first-century A.D. 70. It was unbelieving Jews. The vineyard was taken from them and given to a nation producing the fruit thereof. Let us look at some more Scriptures.

*5 Now will I sing to my wellbeloved a song of my beloved touching his vineyard. My wellbeloved hath a vineyard in a very fruitful hill: 2 **And he fenced it, and gathered out the stones thereof, and planted it with the choicest vine, and built a tower in the midst of it, and also made a winepress therein: and he looked that it should bring forth grapes**, and it brought forth wild grapes. 3 **And now, O inhabitants of Jerusalem, and men of Judah, judge, I pray you, betwixt me and my vineyard. 4 What could have been done more to my vineyard, that I have not done in it?** wherefore, when I looked that it should bring forth grapes, brought it forth wild grapes? 5 And now go to; I will tell you what I will do to my vineyard: **will take away the hedge thereof, and it shall be eaten up; and break*** *down the wall thereof, and it shall be trodden down:_6 And I will lay it waste: it shall not be pruned, nor digged; but there shall come up briers and thorns: I will also command the clouds that they rain no rain upon it. 7 For the vineyard of the Lord of hosts is the house of Israel, and the men of Judah his pleasant plant: and he looked for judgment, but behold oppression; for righteousness, but behold a cry. 8 Woe unto them that join house to house, that lay field to field, till there be no place, that they may be placed alone in the midst of the earth! Isa. 5:1-8 KJV*

Compare these two verses. It is almost a word for word quote.

*33 Hear another parable: There was a certain householder, which planted a vineyard, and **hedged it round about, and digged a winepress in it, and built a tower, and let it out to husbandmen, and went into a far country**: 34 And when the time of the fruit drew near, he sent his servants to the husbandmen, that they might receive the fruits of it. 35 And the husbandmen took his servants, and beat one, and killed another, and stoned another. 36 Again, he sent other servants more than the first: and they did unto them likewise. 37 But last of all he sent unto them his son, saying, They will reverence my son. 38 But when the husbandmen saw the son, they said among themselves, **This is the heir; come, let us kill him, and let us seize on his inheritance**. 39 And they caught him, and cast him out of the vineyard, and slew him. 40 When the lord therefore of the vineyard cometh, what will he do unto those husbandmen? 41 They say unto him, **He will miserably destroy those wicked men, and will let out his vineyard unto other husbandmen, which shall render him the fruits in their seasons**. 42 Jesus saith unto them, Did ye never read in the scriptures, The stone which the builders rejected, the same is become the head of the corner: this is the Lord's doing, and it is marvellous in our eyes? 43 **Therefore say I unto you, The kingdom of God shall be taken from you, and given to a nation bringing forth the fruits thereof.***

*44 And whosoever shall fall on this stone shall be broken: but on whomsoever it shall fall, it will grind him to powder. 45 And when the chief priests and Pharisees had heard his parables, **they perceived that he spake of them**. Matt. 21:33-46 KJV*

Do you see it? He was about to destroy the wicked husbandmen, take the vineyard from them and give it to a nation producing the fruit. They were the ones who crucified the son of the owner of the vineyard. Above Isaiah chapter 5 passage the men of Israel and the house of Judah was the vineyard and his pleasant plant. They were the choicest vine. They were the chosen people. When you compare the Isaiah passage with the Matthew passage you can see very clearly that he was about to remove the hedge and destroy those wicked husbandmen. He would then let out his vineyard unto other husbandmen that would render to him the fruit in season. Then he told them plainly the kingdom is going to be taken from you and given to a nation producing fruit. Yes, the kingdom that was once exclusive to natural Israel is no longer exclusive. It is inclusive. It includes both Jew and Gentile if they are connected to the true vine.

That is what he was trying to tell Nicodemus when he said, you must be born again. He was saying to Nicodemus your natural birth and your natural genealogy is not enough. You must be born again. Many of the parables in the Gospels are telling the same story using different pictures; just like the parable of the rich man and Lazarus was a picture of Jews and Gentiles.

The parable of the sewer is also the same picture. The good seed are the children of the Kingdom. The tares are the children of the wicked one. He told them in that parable to let them both grow together until the harvest. He told them the harvest is the end of the world. But once again this Greek word for *world* is the Greek word *age*. He was telling them the harvest was the end of the old covenant age. He would gather his wheat into the barn and the chaff he would burn with unquenchable fire. Once again that fire came in A.D. 70 and burned up the chaff. All these parables were directed to the house of Israel to give them opportunity to enter the Kingdom. They just, like Esau, sold their birthright for one morsel of meat. See Hebrews chapter 12. God was not excluding the Jews. He was just drawing a bigger circle and saying the only way into the covenants of promise and the blessings of Abraham are through the true vine, which is Jesus Christ.

- God Gives His Son for a Covenant to the People -

*42 **Behold my servant, whom I uphold; mine elect, in whom my soul delighteth; I have put my spirit upon him: he shall bring forth judgment to the Gentiles.** 2 He shall not cry, nor lift up, nor cause his voice to be heard in the street. 3 A bruised reed shall he not break, and the smoking flax shall he not quench: he shall bring forth judgment unto truth. 4 He shall not fail nor be discouraged, till he have set judgment in the earth: and the isles shall wait for his law. 5 Thus saith God the Lord, he that created the heavens, and stretched them out; he that spread forth the earth, and that which cometh out of it; he that giveth breath unto the people upon it, and spirit to them that walk therein: 6 I the Lord have called thee in righteousness, and will hold thine hand, and will keep thee, and **give thee for a covenant of the people, for a light of the Gentiles**; 7 To open the blind eyes, to bring out the prisoners from the prison, and them that sit in darkness out of the prison house. 8 I am the Lord: that is my name: and my glory will I not give to another, neither my praise to graven images. 9 Behold, the former things are come to pass, and new things do I declare: before they spring forth I tell you of them. 10 Sing unto the Lord a new song, and his praise from the end of the earth, ye that go down to the sea, and all that is therein; the isles, and the inhabitants thereof.* Isa. 42:1-10 KJV

This is clearly a messianic prophecy concerning Jesus. Compare these two Scriptures where Jesus quotes from Isaiah.

*17 **That it might be fulfilled which was spoken by Esaias** the prophet, saying, 18 Behold my servant, whom I have chosen; my beloved, in whom my soul is well pleased: I will put my spirit upon him, and he shall shew judgment to the Gentiles. 19 He shall not strive, nor cry; neither shall any man hear his voice in the streets. 20 A bruised reed shall he not break, and smoking flax shall he not quench, till he send forth judgment unto victory. 21 **And in his name shall the Gentiles trust**.* Matt. 12:17-21

Jesus perfectly fulfills these prophecies. His first public message was that he sent me to open the eyes of the blind and set at liberty them that are bruised. He came to be a light to the Gentiles. The people which sat in darkness saw great light. In the Isaiah passage he told them that the former things were about to pass away, and God was about to do a new thing. The new thing was the new covenant. The new song was the new song of the new covenant. It was the new creation that included both Jew and Gentile in Christ, who is the true vine. Jesus Christ is the servant whom he delighted in. God put his Spirit upon him that he might bring judgment to the Gentiles. The mystery which had been hid from ages was about to be revealed, which was Christ in and among all of you. He is the hope of glory. The new covenant is between the Father and the Son and because we are in him, we are included in the covenant.

I believe that is why the gospel of John starts with the Genesis motif. It is because it is not just about God restoring the 12 tribes. It is about God restoring all of creation and bringing them back into relationship with himself. God had chosen the nation of Israel to be the kingdom of priests that would be the vehicle by which he would reach creation. In the new covenant God raised up a priesthood after the order of Melchisedec that was made up of both Jew and Gentile believers. He tore down the middle wall of partition that separated them. Where there is neither Jew nor Greek, bond or free, male nor female, we have been made one in Christ Jesus. A revelation of our inclusive union with him will break down all prejudice. We are now called as a holy nation to fulfill God's mandate to make disciples of all nations. What you serve as a priesthood will draw a line in the sand to determine whether you are an old covenant priest after the order of Levi, or you are a new covenant priest after the order of Melchisedec. If you are an old covenant priest, you will serve up the same fear and judgment. If you are a new covenant priest after the order of Melchisedec, you will serve bread and wine. Bread and wine are the symbols of the covenant table and of the finished work of Jesus Christ. I ask, what are you serving?

- Placement Theology or Replacement Theology -

Before you accuse me a of teaching replacement theology, let us explore more Scripture. Let us see who the Scripture says is Israel.

*22 And thou shalt say unto Pharaoh, Thus saith the Lord, Israel is **my son, even my firstborn**:* Ex. 4:22 KJV

*11 **When Israel was a child, then I loved him, and called my son out of Egypt**. 2 As they called them, so they went from them: they sacrificed unto Baalim, and burned incense to graven images.* Hos. 11:1-2 KJV

Who is Israel in these Old Testament texts? Clearly it is that ancient nation known as Israel which was finally destroyed by the Romans in A.D. 70.

Now let us look at how Matthew treats this same statement. To give the context of this story Joseph and Mary are warned of the Angel of the Lord to flee into Egypt with their family, because Herod sought to kill Jesus. They were instructed to stay there until the death of Herod.

*14 When he arose, he took the young child and his mother by night, and departed into Egypt: 15 And was there until the death of Herod: **that it might be fulfilled which was spoken of the Lord by the prophet, saying, Out of Egypt have I called my son**.* Matt. 2:14-15 KJV

Matthew declares with clarity that Jesus is the true Israel. Jesus was his firstborn. After the death of Herod, he called forth his Son out of Egypt. He is the true vine. Since Jesus is the true Israel and we have been placed in him, then we are the Israel that the below Scripture in Peter is talking about. We are the holy nation and the royal priesthood. Let us compare a couple more Scriptures. God says this to natural Israel:

5 Now therefore, if ye will obey my voice indeed, and keep my covenant, then ye shall be a peculiar treasure unto me above all people: for all the earth is mine: 6 And ye shall be unto me a kingdom of priests, and an holy nation. These are the words which thou shalt speak unto the children of Israel. Ex. 19:5-6 KJV

Peter says this to the church. He uses these exact words:

9 But ye are a chosen generation, a royal priesthood, an holy nation, a peculiar people; that ye should shew forth the praises of him who hath called you out of darkness into his marvellous light: 10 Which in time past were not a people, but are now the people of God: which had not obtained mercy, but now have obtained mercy. 1 Peter 2:9-10 KJV

The apostle Peter leaves no doubt that Christ's followers are chosen for the same purpose for which the nation of Israel was once chosen. Jesus was the seed to whom the original promise was made. Jesus was God's firstborn and out of Egypt have I called my Son. He came back up out of Egypt after the death of Herod to be the fulfillment of the promise to Abraham. He was the fulfillment of the promise to David that, one out of his loins would come. He would never vacate the throne. Jesus did not come to make more promises. He came to fulfill the ones God had spoken throughout the Scriptures. He was the true Tabernacle. He was the true Lamb of God. He was the true Bread that came down from Heaven. He was the true Promise Land. He was the true Israel of God.

I get accused of preaching replacement theology, but I submit to you that replacement theology is a theology the tries to replace Jesus with the national political Israel. But that is not the Israel of God. Jesus is the true Israel of God. He is the *I Am*. I am not replacing Israel with the church. I am replacing the modern nation of Israel with Jesus. Jesus was always the seed to whom the promise was made. See Galatians chapter 3.

- The Blessing of Abraham -

The promise of God to Abraham was, " And I will make of thee a great nation, and I will bless thee, and make thy name great; and thou shalt be a blessing.

3 And I will bless them that bless thee, and curse him that curseth thee: and in thee shall all families of the earth be blessed." Gen. 12:2-3 KJV

That promise was fulfilled in Jesus. The nations are blessed through Jesus.

The great nation that he made was the holy nation called *the church*. Jesus fulfilled the promise that said I will make your name great. We are the children of Abraham by faith in Galatians 3:7. We are, in Christ, the blessing of Abraham that comes upon us through faith. The promise that I will bless them that bless you and curse him that curse you is not to the natural seed of Abraham. It is to those who are in Christ Jesus.

Jesus challenged the scribes and Pharisees when he said to them, if you are Abraham's seed you would believe my word because the children of Abraham are the children of faith. Jesus then told them you are of your father the devil. See John 8:44.

*6 Even as Abraham believed God, and it was accounted to him for righteousness. 7 **Know ye therefore that they which are of faith, the same are the children of Abraham**. 8 And the scripture, foreseeing that God would justify the heathen through faith, preached before the gospel unto Abraham, saying, In thee shall all nations be blessed. 9 So then they which be of faith are blessed with faithful Abraham. 10 For as many as are of the works of the law are under the curse: for it is written, Cursed is every one that continueth not in all things which are written in the book of the law to do them. 11 But that no man is justified by the law in the sight of God, it is evident: for, The just shall live by faith. 12 And the law is not of faith: but, The man that doeth them shall live in them. 13 Christ hath redeemed us from the curse of the law, being made a curse for us: for it is written, Cursed is every one that hangeth on a tree: 14 **That the blessing of Abraham might come on the Gentiles through Jesus Christ**; that we might receive the promise of the Spirit through faith.* Gal. 3:6-14 KJV

*16 Now to Abraham and his seed were the promises made. **He saith not, And to seeds, as of many; but as of one, And to thy seed, which is Christ**.* Gal. 3:16 KJV

The promise was always to the seed of Abraham, but it was made to a specific seed. That seed is Christ. All of God's promises to Abraham would culminate in the person and work of Jesus Christ. He would become the federal head of the true house of Israel. Now the holy nation of God is made up of both Jew and Gentile. There is not two Israels. There is only one. If we as believers are not the Israel of God, then we are not included in the new covenant. The writer of Hebrews said, I will make a new covenant with the house of Israel after those days, saith God. I will write my laws on their hearts and upon their minds, and their sins and iniquities I will remember no more.

*26 For ye are all the children of God by faith in Christ Jesus. 27 For as many of you as have been baptized into Christ have put on Christ. 28 There is neither Jew nor Greek, there is neither bond nor free, there is neither male nor female: for ye are all one in Christ Jesus. 29 **And if ye be Christ's, then are ye Abraham's seed, and heirs according to the promise.** Gal. 3:26-29 KJV*

- You Are Not God's Second Choice -

I used to hear it preached that Israel is God's chosen people whom he really loves. Then bad theology taught us that there was a parenthesis of time where God would take the church to be the Israel of God to make Israel jealous. Then once Israel returned to God, he would once again return to his first love, Israel. That always made me feel like I was his second choice. It is almost as if you are the rebound relationship in the story. As soon as his true love takes him back, he is going to dump us and go back to her. I say to you, **you were his first choice!** You were chosen in Christ before the foundation of the world. The church is not second class and you are not his second choice. You are the love of his life. Let us look at a Scripture in the Amplified Bible because it tells us that the slave woman and her son **will never** be an heir and share in the inheritance with the son of the free woman. In the verses below we will see that the old Jerusalem represented the old covenant. The Jerusalem which is above the messianic Kingdom of God is the free woman.

21 Tell me, you who are bent on being under the Law, will you listen to what the Law [really] says? 22 For it is written that Abraham had two sons, one by the bondmaid and one by the free woman. [Gen 16:15; 21:2,9.] 23 But whereas the child of the slave woman was born according to the flesh and had an ordinary birth, the son of the free woman was born in fulfillment of the promise. 24 **Now all this is an allegory; these [two women] represent two covenants.** One covenant originated from Mount Sinai [where the Law was given] and bears [children destined] for slavery; this is Hagar. 25 **Now Hagar is (stands for) Mount Sinai in Arabia and she corresponds to and belongs in the same category with the present Jerusalem, for she is in bondage together with her children.** 26 **But the Jerusalem above (the Messianic kingdom of Christ) is free, and she is our mother.** 27 For it is written in the Scriptures, Rejoice, O barren woman, who has not given birth to children; break forth into a joyful shout, you who are not feeling birth pangs, for the desolate woman has many more children than she who has a husband. [Isa 54:1.] 28 **But we, brethren, are children [not by physical descent, as was Ishmael, but] like Isaac, born in virtue of promise.** 29 Yet [just] as at that time the child [of ordinary birth] born according to the flesh despised and persecuted him [who was born remarkably] according to [the promise and the working of] the [Holy] Spirit, so it is now also. [Gen 21:9.] 30 **But what does the Scripture say? Cast out and send away the slave woman and her son, for never shall the son of the slave woman be heir and share the inheritance with the son of the free woman.** [Gen 21:10.] 31 **So, brethren, we [who are born again] are not children of a slave woman [the natural], but of the free [the supernatural].** Gal. 4:21-31 AMP

I do not know how you could make it any clearer. It is not by natural descent. Once again, let me say that I am not anti-Semitic. I am just pro-Jesus. I am not anti-anything. I am simply saying to you that there is only one way into the covenant of promise and that is through faith in Christ and his finished work. The Old Testament Scriptures that speak of the restoration of the Israel can only find their fulfillment in Christ. There is no other name given under heaven whereby men must be saved. That name is the name of Jesus and he is truly the great *I Am*. I know I am using a lot of Scripture in this chapter, but I think it is particularly important to see it for yourself.

28 For he is not a Jew, which is one outwardly; neither is that circumcision, which is outward in the flesh: 29 But he is a Jew, which is one inwardly; and circumcision is that of the heart, in the spirit, and not in the letter; whose praise is not of men, but of God. Rom. 2:28-29 KJV

In the next several chapters in the book of Romans, he continues to reiterate that Abraham was justified by faith and continues to affirm that access into this grace and inheritance is through faith and faith alone.

16 Therefore it is of faith, that it might be by grace; to the end the promise might be sure to all the seed; not to that only which is of the law, but to that also which is of the faith of Abraham; who is the father of us all, 17 (As it is written, I have made thee a father of many nations,) before him whom he believed, even God, who quickeneth the dead, and calleth those things which be not as though they were. Rom. 4:16-17 KJV

*6 Not as though the word of God hath taken none effect. **For they are not all Israel, which are of Israel**: 7 Neither, because they are the seed of Abraham, are they all children: but, In Isaac shall thy seed be called. 8 **That is, They which are the children of the flesh, these are not the children of God**: but the children of the promise are counted for the seed.* Rom. 9:6-8 KJV

He tells them in the end of Romans chapter 9 that though the number of the children of Israel be as the sand of the sea, a remnant shall be saved. Paul is talking in this text about a remnant of the natural Israel who would believe in Jesus, would become part of the household of faith and be a part of the true Israel of God.

- All Israel Will Be Saved -

In Romans chapter 11 it said, all Israel will be saved. The *all Israel* that will be saved will be the Israel that is in Christ. If that is not true, then these two Scriptures are in conflict, because Romans chapter 9 says, a remnant will be saved. I submit to you that the remnant is the remnant out of old covenant Israel that were believers and have been brought into Christ through faith. Christ is the fulfillment of all the promises God made to the

156

fathers. For in Christ all of God's promises are yes and amen.

Romans chapter 11 opens with the question, has God cast away his people? His answer is, God has not cast away his people which he foreknew. The gift and call of God are irrevocable. Then he repeats the fact that there would be a remnant according to the election of grace. In other words, the only branches he is going cut off is unbelieving natural Israel; those Jews who did not attain the promises through faith.

Remember, the book of John was written so that you might believe that Jesus is the Christ, and that believing you would have life through his name. The line that is being drawn in the sand is not, are you a Jew or a Gentile. The line in the sand that has been drawn is, are you a believer or an unbeliever. Blindness in part happened to Israel because God wanted to include all men. The Gentiles were included to provoke Israel to jealousy, not so God would leave us and go back to them, but so they would leave their apostasy and come back to him. The door is open to every individual Jew or Gentile, or any ethnic group of people. But there is only one door and Jesus said, "I am the door into the sheepfold."

*14 If by any means I may provoke to emulation them which are my flesh, and might **save some of them**. 15 For if the casting away of them be the reconciling of the world, what shall the receiving of them be, but life from the dead? 16 For if the firstfruit be holy, the lump is also holy: and if the root be holy, so are the branches. 17 **And if some of the branches be broken off**, and thou, being a wild olive tree, wert graffed in among them, and with them partakest of the root and fatness of the olive tree; 18 Boast not against the branches. But if thou boast, thou bearest not the root, but the root thee. 19 Thou wilt say then, The branches were broken off, that I might be grafted in. 20 Well; because of unbelief they were broken off, and thou standest by faith. Be not highminded, but fear: 21 For if God spared not the natural branches, take heed lest he also spare not thee. 22 Behold therefore the goodness and severity of God: on them which fell, severity; but toward thee, goodness, if thou continue in his goodness: otherwise thou also shalt be cut off. 23 **And they also, if they abide not still in unbelief, shall be grafted in: for God is able to graft them in again**. 24 For* *if thou wert cut out of the olive tree which is wild by nature, and wert grafted contrary to nature into a good olive tree: how much more shall these, which be the natural branches, be grafted into their own olive tree? 25 For I would not, brethren, that ye should be ignorant of this mystery, lest ye should be wise in your own conceits; that blindness in part is happened to Israel, until the fulness of the Gentiles be come in. 26 And so all Israel shall be saved: as it is written, There shall come out of Sion the Deliverer, and shall turn away ungodliness from Jacob: 27 For this is my covenant unto them, when I shall take away their sins. 28 As concerning the gospel, they are enemies for your sakes: **but as touching the election, they are beloved for the fathers' sakes. 29 For the gifts and calling of God are without repentance**. 30 For as ye in times past have not believed God, yet have now obtained mercy through their unbelief: 31 Even so have these also now not believed, that through your mercy they also may obtain mercy. 32 For God hath concluded them all in unbelief, that he might have mercy upon all.* Rom. 11:14-32 KJV

The focus of this chapter is not on the branches, it is on the root. Jesus Christ is the root and the offspring of David. See Revelation 22:16. If you are connected to the right root you will produce the right fruit. The point I am making here is that Israel is not the true vine. Jesus said, "I am the true vine". It does not matter if you are a natural brand or you are a grafted in branch. The issue is what you are grafted into.

In John chapter 15 Jesus said, every branch in me that does not bear fruit is taken away. The branches that were taken away are described in this chapter as the natural branches, because they did not abide in the vine to bring forth fruit. They were indeed cast forth and cast into the fire and burned. This is not talking about something in the future. This is talking about what happened in A.D. 70. The power of the holy people was finally broken, and Jerusalem was like a plowed field. The city was burned to the ground and not one stone was left upon another that was not thrown down. Their exclusive covenant with Jehovah under the law was no longer in force. God would make a new covenant that would be inclusive. It would include both Jew and Gentile so that all Israel would be saved. That is, every one that is in Christ. Remember, Israel is my firstborn and out of Egypt have I called my Son. The true Israel of God is Jesus. The book of Galatians calls the covenant of the law a temporary covenant. The law was added because of transgression, UNTIL the seed should come to whom the promise was made. That mosaic covenant could not disannul the original covenant that God made with Abraham based on faith.

16 Now to Abraham and his seed were the promises made. He saith not, And to seeds, as of many; but as of one, And to thy seed, which is Christ. 17 **And this I say, that the covenant, that was confirmed before of God in Christ, the law, which was four hundred and thirty years after, cannot disannul, that it should make the promise of none effect.** *18 For if the inheritance be of the law, it is no more of promise: but God gave it to Abraham by promise. 19 Wherefore then serveth the law? It was added because of transgressions,* **till the seed should come to whom the promise was made;** *and it was ordained by angels in the hand of a mediator.* Gal. 3:16-19 KJV

- Conclusion -

I hope this book has helped you to move from the shadow to substance, from the type and shadow to reality. I hope it has helped you learn the language of the Spirit and how God uses symbolism and types and shadows to speak to his people. It is these things that help us to communicate the Gospel. Remember, the apostles did not have the New Testament from which to preach. They preached Christ from the law and the prophets because in the volume of the book it was written about him. Yes, they thought the natural temple was what God was looking for, but that is not the temple for which God was looking. The many membered body of Christ is the true tabernacle which the Lord pitched and not man. God has made his home in men.

Nicodemus thought his natural birth was enough, but Jesus said to him, you must be born again. There is a new birth. You thought Moses and the law was the light, but that is not the light. Jesus said, I am the light of the world. You thought the manna that fell in the wilderness was the true bread, but that is not the true bread that came down from Heaven. Jesus said, I am the true bread that came down from Heaven. You thought performance Christianity was the door into the sheepfold, but that is not the door. Jesus is the door. You thought the wicked shepherds of Israel were the good shepherds, but they were not the true Shepherd of the sheep. Jesus said, I am the good Shepherd. You thought the way into life was through searching the old covenant Scriptures, but they were they which testify of Jesus who said, I am the resurrection and the life.

Jesus said, I am the way the truth and the life and no man can come to the Father except through me. Jesus is the way to the Father. You thought Israel was the true vine, but they are not the true vine. Jesus is the vine and we are the branches. You thought natural Israel was the Israel of God, but that is not the Israel of God. Jesus is the Israel of God, and we are part of that by virtue of our union with him. You thought old Jerusalem was God's capital city, but it was Mount Sinai in Arabia which spoke of old covenant natural Jerusalem who is in bondage with her children to this day still under the law. That is not the true Jerusalem. The true Jerusalem is the Messianic Kingdom of Christ, of which we are part.

Do you see it? Everything points to Christ. For he truly is **The Great I Am!** I am what I am by the grace of God. Right believing will produce right living. Faith will replace fear. Love will replace law. You will begin to recover your life as you make the transition from an old covenant paradigm to a new covenant life in Christ. You will discover the abundant life on every level. You will experience the days of heaven on earth as you realize the promise land is not a place, it is a person named Jesus. You will no longer live like strangers right in the land of promise. From your position in Christ you will become a land that flows with milk and honey. Remember, the apostle John said, "But these things are written, that you might believe that Jesus is the Christ, and that believing you would have life through his name." John 20:31 KJV

~ The End ~

CONTACT THE AUTHOR

Lynn Hiles Ministries P.O. Box 127 Great Cacapon, WV 25422

Phone: 304-579-5336
Email: info@lynnhiles.com
Web: www.lynnhiles.com

This book and all other books and materials by Dr. Lynn Hiles are available at www.lynnhiles.com or by phone at 304-579-5336.

Additional Titles By Dr. Lynn Hiles

God's Beauty and the Beast

The Revelation of Jesus Christ

Unforced Rhythms of Grace

From Law To Grace

Made in the USA
Middletown, DE
14 September 2021